PMI Project Management Salary Survey

2000 Edition

PMI Project Management Salary Survey

2000 Edition

Project Management Institute
Newtown Square, Pennsylvania USA

Library of Congress Cataloging-in-Publication Data

PMI project management salary survey
     p.   cm.
  ISBN 1-880410-26-5
  1. Executives--Salaries, etc.--United States--Statistics. 2. Industrial project
management--Statistics. I. Project Management Institute.

HD4965.5.U6 P56 2000
331.2'81658404'0973--dc21   00-066470
                                         CIP
  ISBN: 1-880410-26-5

Published by: Project Management Institute, Inc.
                Four Campus Boulevard
                Newtown Square, Pennsylvania 19073-3299 USA
                Phone: 610-356-4600 or Visit our website: www.pmi.org
                E-mail: pmihq@pmi.org

10   9   8   7   6   5   4   3   2   1

Contents

Contents

Introduction

Introduction

The purpose of the *PMI Project Management Salary Survey* 2000 Edition is to establish normative compensation and benefits data for the project management profession on a global basis. Data for this study was collected via a worldwide mail survey of a random sample of Project Management Institute (PMI®) members. Information generated by this study can be utilized by individuals engaged in any aspect of, or position within, the project management profession. Additionally, information within this study can be utilized by human resource managers and other individuals in companies or other organizations who are concerned about establishing appropriate levels of compensation and benefits for employees engaged in any aspect of project management.

The *PMI Project Management Salary Survey* 2000 Edition is a product of PMI, which serves over 70,000 individuals engaged in project management throughout the world. PMI is a 501 (c) 6 not-for-profit global professional association founded in 1969 and dedicated to advancing the state of the art in project management. PMI establishes project management standards, provides professional certification, offers seminars and educational programs, conducts research, publishes project management books and periodicals, and offers numerous other member and professional benefits.

The *PMI Project Management Salary Survey* 2000 Edition provides salary, bonus/overtime, and deferred compensation information for specific job titles/positions within the project management profession. The study also contains normative data for a comprehensive list of benefits and an array of other relevant parameters. Information is presented on a global basis and, where appropriate, information by regions of the world is presented. Readers who are interested in comparing their personal compensation and benefits to data contained in this study may wish to check several different tables.

The *PMI Project Management Salary Survey* 2000 Edition was commissioned by PMI. Operational aspects of the research design and analysis were conducted by Kerr & Downs Research (www.kerr-downs.com).

Format of the Report

The Executive Summary follows this section of the report. The first major section of the study (pages 39 through 146) contains compensation information from individuals working in the project management profession throughout the world. Information about benefits is contained in pages 147 through 161. The final major section of the report beginning on page 163 contains profile information on individuals who responded to the study.

Interpretation of Compensation Data

Compensation information was reported by individuals either in United States dollars or in their countries' currencies. Compensation data were converted to United States dollars in two ways: 1) by utilizing official exchange rate information from the first day of the data-collection period (1 April 2000), and 2) by utilizing purchasing power parities (PPPs) from the Organisation for Economic Co-Operation & Development (OECD)*. PPPs are rates of currency conversion that equalize purchasing power of different currencies by eliminating differences in price levels between countries. In their simplest form, PPPs are simply price relatives that show the ratio of prices in national currencies for the same good or service in different countries. For example, if the price of cauliflower in France is 8.00 francs and in the United States it is 1.50 dollars, then the PPP for cauliflower between France and the United States is 8.00 francs to 1.50 dollars or 5.33 francs to the dollar. This means that for every dollar spent on cauliflower in the United States, 5.33 francs would have to be spent in France to obtain the same quantity and quality of cauliflower.

All compensation data are presented in dual tables: 1) by exchange rate conversion and 2) by PPP conversion. To simplify text throughout the report, nearly all text relates to compensation information converted by exchange rates because of the rates' common use worldwide.

All compensation data in the study have been converted to the United States dollar because 75% of PMI members are from the United States.

In some sections, comparisons are made to data in the *Project Management Salary Survey* 1996 Edition.

* OECD has not developed purchasing power parities for all countries.

Format of the Report

Geographic Areas of the World

Compensation data are shown in the report for the following geographic areas:

Geographical Areas*

United States	*Europe*	*Latin America*
United States	Austria	Argentina
	Belgium	Brazil
Canada	Czech Republic	Caribbean
Canada	Denmark	Chile
	Finland	Columbia
Asia	France	Jamaica
China	Germany	Mexico
Hong Kong PRC	Ireland	Panama
India	Italy	Puerto Rico
Indonesia	Netherlands	Venezuela
Japan	Serbia	
Korea	Slovenia	*Middle East*
Malaysia	Spain	Cyprus
Philippines	Sweden	Egypt
Singapore	Switzerland	Iran
Thailand	United Kingdom	Israel
		Kuwait
Australia/New Zealand		Oman
Australia		Saudi Arabia
New Zealand		Turkey
		United Arab Emirates

* All countries shown had at least one PMI member who responded to the study. The sample size of respondents from Africa was too small for a geographic area breakdown, but the responses were included in the global data.

Format of the Report

United States Regions

Northeast
Connecticut
Delaware
District of Columbia
Maine
Maryland
Massachusetts
New Hampshire
New Jersey
New York
Pennsylvania
Rhode Island
Vermont

Midwest
Illinois
Indiana
Iowa
Michigan
Minnesota
Ohio
Wisconsin

Southeast
Alabama
Arkansas
Florida
Georgia
Kentucky
Louisiana
Mississippi
Missouri
North Carolina
South Carolina
Tennessee
Virginia
West Virginia

Southwest
Arizona
New Mexico
Texas

Plains/Mountain
Colorado
Idaho
Kansas
Montana
Nebraska
North Dakota
Oklahoma
South Dakota
Utah
Wyoming

Far West
Alaska
California
Hawaii
Nevada
Oregon
Washington

Canada Regions (Provinces)
Alberta
British Columbia
Nova Scotia
Ontario
Quebec
Saskatchewan
Other

While there are many different ways to divide countries and regions of the world, the preceding areas were chosen primarily based on the need to have adequate responses to generate valid compensation and benefits information.

Format of the Report

Validity of Compensation and Benefits Information

The validity of data in this report is impacted by sample sizes. On a global basis, the sample size of 1,290 provides reliability and stability of the data. Compensation and benefits data are presented in the report *if at least ten individuals* provided information. That is, no information (as denoted by --) is shown in this report unless there were at least ten respondents for a given location, job title, level of responsibility, industry affiliation, etc. While the number ten is strictly arbitrary, it does assure respondent anonymity and guarantees some level of stability in the data. However, the reader should note that this study presents results based on self-reported data. And it should be noted that because of the detailed level of analysis, in many cases, sample sizes are small. The impact of unusual values on summary statistics such as means and medians is greater when there are comparatively few data points. Sample sizes are reported in all tables by using the symbol "N." Larger sample sizes result in more stable normative data.

Reporting of Compensation Data

Each table that shows compensation data presents the following elements of information:

25th percentile -	the value above which 75% of individuals earned more. For example, the 25th percentile for total compensation was $55,100, that is, 75% of individuals earned more than $55,100 in total compensation.
Median -	the value at which half of individuals earned more and half earned less. For example, the 50th percentile for total compensation was $75,000; that is, 50% of individuals earned more, and 50% earned less.
75th percentile -	the value above which 25% of individuals earned more. For example, the 75th percentile for total compensation was $95,200; that is, 25% of individuals earned more than $95,200.
Mean or average -	the arithmetic average of a series of numbers. For example, the average of $50,000, $60,000, and $70,000 is $60,000. The mean total compensation was $82,389.

The median (also referred to as the 50th percentile) and the mean (average) are measures of central tendency. That is, they are specific figures that summarize a distribution or series of numbers. The mean (average) can be affected by unusually large or small numbers. For example, the mean of $50,000,

Format of the Report

$60,000, and $190,000 is $100,000. The median (50th percentile) of these same three numbers would be reported as $60,000. Normally, the median and mean values will be between the 25th and 75th percentiles. In a few cases in this study, unusually high compensation for one or a few individuals have resulted in mean values that are greater than the 75th percentile.

Targets of Analysis

Compensation and benefits information are shown on a global basis and are shown for levels of each of the following:

Geographic Location - as listed on pages 5 through 6

Employment Status
> Full-time employed
> Full-time self-employed

Hours Worked Per Week
> 1–40 hours
> 41–45 hours
> 46–50 hours
> 51–55 hours
> 56–60 hours
> 61+ hours

Job/Position Title
> CEO, CFO, CIO, etc.
> Senior Management
> Director of Project/Program Management
> Program Manager
> Project Manager
> Project Management/Consultant/Advisor
> Project Engineer
> Project Team Leader
> Project Coordinator
> Project Planner/Scheduler

Format of the Report

Industry Affiliation

Construction
    Commercial/Heavy Industrial
    Residential
    Other Construction
Other Business Activities
    Academia
    Aerospace
    Architecture/Design
    Automation Services
    Business Management
    Computers/Software/Data Processing (DP)
    Consulting
    Defense
    E-Business
    Economics/Finance
    Education/Training
    Environmental/Waste/Sewage
    Engineering
    Financial Services
    Health/Human/Social Services
    Information Technology
    International Development
    Legal

Other Business Activities (cont.)
    Printing/Publishing
    Public Administration/Government
    Real Estate/Insurance
    Supply Chain
    Systems Security
    Telecommunications
    Transportation
    Urban Development
    Utilities
    Web Technology
    Other Business Activities
Resources
    Coal/Gas/Oil
Manufacturing
    Automotive
    Chemical
    Electrical/Electronic
    Food
    Machinery/Metals
    Petroleum
    Pharmaceutical
    Other Manufacturing

Format of the Report

Role in Organization

Engineering
  Civil
  Electrical
  Electronics
  Environment
  Industrial
  Mechanical
  Other Engineering

Management
  Communications
  Configuration
  Contract/Procurement
  Corporate/Administrative
  Cost
  Critical Chain
  Earned Value
  Human Resources
  Information/Computer
  Materials

Management (cont.)
  Project/Program
  Quality
  Records
  Risk/Safety
  Scope/Technical
  Site/Facility
  Time Management/Scheduling/Planning

Other
  Consulting
  Finance
  Marketing/Business Development/Sales
  Production
  Project Accounting/Audit
  Research/Product Development
  Service & Outsourcing
  Teaching/Training
  Web Strategist/Technologist
  Other

Format of the Report

Scope of Responsibilities

Level 1	Accountable for the strategy and performance of the overall organization or division.
Level 2	Direct responsibility of total program execution. The program typically requires accountability for a related series of projects, executed over a broad period of time, which is designed to accomplish broad goals of the program to which these individual projects contribute.
Level 3	Responsible for directing large projects or a multitude of smaller projects. Manage all aspects of project, from beginning to end, with direct accountability for project execution while leading a team, or teams, to accomplish specific objectives in a given time frame and with limited resources.
Level 4	Work within or outside of a project or program office providing support, training, and consultation to project managers and the organization. Provide support to the project or program office and facilitate process implementation.
Level 5	Combine technical expertise essential to project execution, with management of project task(s) implementation while leading task specialists.
Level 6	Typically report to Project Manager and run certain segments or critical work packages of the project. Exceptional technical capabilities and leadership role for 3–4-person teams.
Level 7	Responsible for coordinating technical activities associated with the assigned project. Usually a technical specialist residing within the organization who is not normally held accountable for the project.
Level 8	Administer or supervise support services for project. Develop, implement, and maintain project management information system that provides adequate information with which to manage the project.
Level 9	Track, coordinate, and publish detailed planning and scheduling for the project.
Level 10	Team member from a functional department or project office with recognized specialty or "expert" status within the respective organization. Function as an individual contributor or serve as an interface with other specialists in respective departments.
Level 11	None of the above applies to me.

Format of the Report

Scope of Projects

    Local
    State/province
    Multi-state
    Within one country
    Multiple countries
    Multiple continents

Mean Budget Size of Projects (all figures are in United States dollars)

    <$100,000
    $100,000 - $249,999
    $250,000 - $499,999
    $500,000 - $999,999
    $1.0 million - $1.99 million
    $2.0 million - $2.99 million
    $3.0 million - $3.99 million
    $4.0 million - $4.99 million
    $5.0 million - $9.99 million
    $10.0 million - $24.99 million
    $25.0 million - $49.99 million
    $50.0 million - $99.99 million
    $100.0 million - $499.99 million
    $500.0 million - $999.99 million
    $1.0 billion - $9.99 billion
    $\geq$ $10.0 billion

Number of Projects Engaged In/Managed

    1 project
    2 projects
    3 projects
    4 projects
    5 projects
    6 - 10 projects
    11+ projects

Number of Employees Supervised

    1 - 2 people
    3 - 4 people
    5 - 6 people
    7 - 8 people
    9 - 10 people
    11 - 15 people
    16 - 20 people
    21 - 25 people
    26 - 50 people
    51+ people

Number of People in Project Management at Location

    1 - 2 people
    3 - 4 people
    5 - 10 people
    11 - 15 people
    16 - 20 people
    21 - 30 people
    31+ people

Number of People in Project Management in Organization

    1 - 10 people
    11 - 25 people
    26 - 50 people
    51 - 100 people
    101 - 300 people
    300+ people

Number of Employees at Location

    1 - 10 people
    11 - 20 people
    21 - 50 people
    51 - 100 people
    101 - 200 people
    201 - 500 people
    501 - 1,000 people
    1,001+ people

Format of the Report

Number of Employees in Organization

    1 - 50 people
    51 - 100 people
    101 - 200 people
    201 - 500 people
    501 - 1,000 people
    1,001 - 5,000 people
    5,001 - 10,000 people
    10,001 - 20,000 people
    20,001+ people

Number of Years in Project Management

    1 - 2 years
    3 - 5 years
    6 - 10 years
    11 - 15 years
    16 - 20 years
    21+ years

Number of Years Worked for Current Employer

    1 year
    2 years
    3 - 5 years
    6 - 10 years
    11 - 15 years
    16 - 20 years
    21+ years

Project Management Professional
(PMP®) Certification

    PMP
    Non PMP

Gender
    Male
    Female

Age
    25 years or less
    25–34 years
    35–44 years
    45–54 years
    55–64 years

Education

    High school degree or equivalent
    Some college/AA degree or equivalent
    College (undergraduate) degree or equivalent
    Master's degree or equivalent
    Doctoral degree or equivalent

Benefits

Individuals in the study indicated which of the following benefits were included in their total compensation and benefits packages:

    Insurance
        Healthcare
        Long-term disability
        Short-term disability
        Accidental death
        Vision
        Prescription drugs
        Dental
        Life
        Professional liability
        Other insurance

    Insurance delivery/format
        Standard plan
        Cafeteria plan

Format of the Report

Benefits
      Retirement contributions by employer
      Performance incentive
      Retention incentive
      Signing bonus
      Stock options
      Relocation/travel bonus
      Holiday bonus
      Housing allowance/free housing
      Free participation in stock purchases
      Vehicle
      Entertainment allowance
      Club memberships
      Tickets to events
      At-risk bonus pay
      Mortgage paid by employer until current house is sold
      Other benefits
      Paid child care
      Maternity/paternity leave
      Matched savings
      Sabbatical with pay
      Wellness program
      Free parking
      Adult dependent care
      Cellular telephone
      Laptop/home computer
      Reimbursement of academic tuition
      Reimbursement of professional seminars/workshops
      Reimbursement of professional association dues
      Presence of retirement plan
      Type of retirement plan
      Vesting period for retirement plan
      Number of paid vacation days
      Number of paid sick days
      Number of paid holidays
      Number of paid personal days

Executive Summary

Executive Summary

Introduction

The *PMI Project Management Salary Survey* 2000 Edition reports normative compensation and benefits information for the project management industry. Results within this report are based on responses from 1,290 Project Management Institute (PMI) members worldwide. Information was collected via mail surveys of randomly selected PMI members during April and May 2000.

Based on 1,290 responses to this study from PMI members, the typical respondent:

- Lives in the United States (58%)
- Is full-time employed by an organization (92%)
- Works 41–50 hours per week (56%)
- Is a project or program manager (52%)
- Works for an organization affiliated with information technology (28%), consulting (20%), or computers/software/DP (19%)
- Has role within an organization in project/program management (61%)
- Has a mean budget size of less than $2.0 million for the typical project that he engaged in/ managed (50%)
- Engaged in/managed 3 or fewer projects (52%)
- Presently supervises 10 or fewer people (50%)
- Has more than 10 employees in project/program management at her location (51%)
- Has more than 25 employees (64%) in project/program management in his organization
- Has more than 100 employees at her office, location, or division (53%)
- Has more than 1,000 employees in his entire organization (56%)
- Has worked in project management more than 5 years (70%)
- Has worked for her current employer more than 5 years (50%)
- Has not earned PMP® certification (64%)
- Has a retirement plan (84%)
- Receives retirement contributions from his employer (76%)
- Receives approximately 19 vacation days annually
- Works in a traditional office (84%) and works 5 days a month away from the office
- Has a clear, informal or unstated career path (68%)
- Has not relocated with the same employer in the last 5 years (69%)
- Is 35–54 years old (74%)
- Has a college (undergraduate) degree (46%) or a master's degree (39%)
- Is male (75%)
- Has been a PMI member for 1 or 2 years (63%)
- Has healthcare (92%), life (76%), and long-term disability (79%) insurance
- Receives retirement contributions from her employer (76%)
- Has an annual mean total compensation of $82,389 (US)
- Has an annual median total compensation of $75,000 (US)
- Has professional association dues reimbursed by employer (97%)

Executive Summary

Total Compensation

Total Compensation by Region of the World

Median and mean total compensation for regions of the world are shown below (all figures are in United States dollars and are based on conversions by exchange rates):

Region	Mean Total Compensation	Median Total Compensation
Global	$82,389	$75,000
United States	$87,807	$81,115
Canada	$61,614	$52,814
Asia	$111,883	$93,025
Australia/New Zealand	$62,334	$50,000
Europe	$73,879	$66,529
Latin America	$79,157	$62,517
Middle East	$68,608	$62,500

Total Compensation within the United States

Region	Mean Total Compensation	Median Total Compensation
Northeast	$90,158	$85,500
Midwest	$84,299	$80,000
Southeast	$81,960	$78,000
Southwest	$81,987	$77,000
Plains/Mountain	$88,507	$81,125
Far West	$103,595	$83,000

Total Compensation within Canada

Province	Mean Total Compensation	Median Total Compensation
Alberta	$61,184	$52,814
British Columbia	$56,621	$49,801
Nova Scotia	$66,535	$46,043
Ontario	$61,343	$56,876
Quebec	$61,254	$51,676
Saskatchewan	$62,245	$54,845
Other	$65,986	$53,000

Executive Summary

Compensation figures on pages 19 through 25 are global data.

Total Compensation by Employment Status

Employment Status	Mean Total Compensation	Median Total Compensation
Full-time employed	$81,104	$74,482
Full-time self-employed	$109,122	$92,000

Total Compensation by Hours Worked

Hours Worked	Mean Total Compensation	Median Total Compensation
1 - 40 Hours	$71,475	$63,250
41 - 45 Hours	$75,680	$72,797
46 - 50 Hours	$89,061	$80,000
51 - 55 Hours	$82,474	$80,000
56 - 60 Hours	$105,269	$85,999
61+ Hours	$103,110	$88,682

Total Compensation by Title

Title	Mean Total Compensation	Median Total Compensation
CEO, CFO, CIO, etc.	$134,195	$98,780
Senior Management	$117,935	$90,000
Director of Project/Program Management	$97,080	$94,000
Program Manager	$88,465	$86,000
Project Manager	$73,648	$68,715
Project Management Consultant/Advisor	$83,544	$79,422
Project Engineer	$60,570	$61,500
Project Team Leader	$64,192	$66,185
Project Coordinator	$55,908	$47,000
Project Planner/Scheduler	$65,872	$74,100
Project Team Member	$125,236	$58,600

Executive Summary

Total Compensation by Industry Affiliation

Industry Affiliation	Mean Total Compensation	Median Total Compensation
Construction		
Commercial/Heavy Industrial	$84,033	$80,000
Residential	$71,479	$61,893
Other Construction	$77,261	$78,500
Other Business Activities		
Academia	$67,318	$49,000
Aerospace	$84,618	$84,000
Architecture/Design	$75,565	$63,758
Automation Services	$66,373	$59,594
Business Management	$91,576	$77,500
Computers/Software/DP	$89,039	$81,000
Consulting	$92,371	$82,000
Defense	$73,004	$71,500
E-Business	$92,665	$77,000
Economics/Finance	$94,981	$75,000
Education/Training	$86,488	$80,000
Environmental/Waste/Sewage	$81,865	$80,184
Engineering	$84,244	$79,460
Financial Services	$78,315	$74,000
Health/Human/Social Services	$68,512	$60,000
Information Technology	$87,339	$75,000
International Development	$104,967	$93,000
Public Administration/Government	$70,360	$65,000
Real Estate/Insurance	$74,680	$73,250
Supply Chain	$88,469	$80,000
Systems Security	$75,995	$69,000
Telecommunications	$75,898	$71,547
Transportation	$87,201	$81,500
Urban Development	$86,582	$78,425
Utilities	$101,192	$80,934
Web Technology	$103,733	$79,460
Other Business Activities	$69,646	$66,734
Resources		
Coal/Glass/Oil	$93,904	$80,184
Manufacturing		
Automotive	$99,924	$83,250
Chemical	$101,290	$91,000
Electrical/Electronic	$111,802	$83,500
Food	$82,395	$80,684
Machinery/Metals	$76,843	$60,000
Petroleum	$84,927	$78,225
Pharmaceutical	$94,313	$86,000
Other Manufacturing	$82,198	$74,150

Executive Summary

Total Compensation by Role in Organization

Role in Organization	Mean Total Compensation	Median Total Compensation
Engineering		
Civil	$84,187	$73,150
Electrical	$87,097	$60,535
Electronics	$76,725	$79,684
Environment	$72,780	$70,000
Industrial	$88,435	$77,684
Mechanical	$81,067	$80,000
Other Engineering	$74,278	$65,600
Management		
Communications	$83,610	$76,000
Configuration	$95,490	$79,422
Contract/Procurement	$84,941	$80,000
Corporate/Administrative	$98,134	$80,000
Cost	$83,198	$79,422
Critical Chain	$85,268	$81,184
Earned Value	$95,644	$85,999
Human Resources	$97,963	$80,000
Information/Computer	$80,174	$76,925
Materials	$69,994	$68,999
Project/Program	$81,273	$73,000
Quality	$77,991	$76,000
Records	$79,244	$61,440
Risk/Safety	$86,906	$81,184
Scope/Technical	$78,475	$68,999
Site/Facility	$79,293	$70,000
Time Management/Scheduling/Planning	$78,237	$74,200
Other		
Consulting	$91,373	$80,368
Finance	$69,663	$70,000
Marketing/Business Development/Sales	$87,263	$75,000
Production	$68,591	$62,500
Project Accounting/Audit	$72,031	$56,876
Research/Product Development	$81,469	$71,863
Service & Outsourcing	$80,589	$68,734
Teaching/Training	$74,753	$62,500
Web Strategist/Technologist	$64,539	$62,500
Other	$76,979	$80,000

Executive Summary

Total Compensation by Scope of Responsibilities

Scope of Responsibilities (see page 11)	Mean Total Compensation	Median Total Compensation
Level 1	$118,876	$90,000
Level 2	$92,604	$88,300
Level 3	$76,928	$72,500
Level 4	$82,741	$78,187
Level 5	$69,827	$67,500
Level 6	$74,093	$76,083
Level 7	$64,733	$70,000
Level 8	$57,588	$55,650
Level 9	$67,224	$67,520
Level 10	$96,605	$63,000
Level 11	$64,238	$62,500

Total Compensation by Geographic Scope of Projects

Geographic Scope of Projects	Mean Total Compensation	Median Total Compensation
Local	$75,818	$70,000
State/Province	$78,671	$69,000
Multi-State/Province	$82,653	$76,000
Within One Country	$78,307	$71,048
Multiple Countries	$91,701	$80,000
Multiple Continents	$90,948	$83,000

Total Compensation by Average Budget Size of Projects

Mean Budget Size of Projects	Mean Total Compensation	Median Total Compensation
<$100,000	$68,434	$62,000
$100,000 - $249,999	$71,257	$70,000
$250,000 - $499,999	$72,174	$63,527
$500,000 - $999,999	$78,823	$75,580
$1.0 Million - $1.99 Million	$77,218	$75,000
$2.0 Million - $2.99 Million	$83,009	$78,600
$3.0 Million - $3.99 Million	$80,201	$76,000
$4.0 Million - $4.99 Million	$84,167	$88,000
$5.0 Million - $9.99 Million	$86,656	$78,000
$10.0 Million - $24.99 Million	$89,597	$82,000
$25.0 Million - $49.99 Million	$87,955	$80,000
$50.0 Million - $99.99 Million	$99,601	$81,500
$100.0 Million - $499.99 Million	$120,532	$90,000
$500.0 Million - $999.99 Million	$92,055	$80,000
$1.0 Billion - $9.99 Billion	$90,719	$88,000

Executive Summary

Total Compensation by Number of Projects Engaged In/Managed

Number of Projects Engaged In/Managed	Mean Total Compensation	Median Total Compensation
1 Project	$80,119	$75,000
2 Projects	$81,977	$71,000
3 Projects	$86,928	$75,000
4 Projects	$74,230	$70,000
5 Projects	$78,656	$80,184
6 - 10 Projects	$86,721	$78,000
11+ Projects	$86,437	$75,159

Total Compensation by Number of Employees Supervised

Number of Employees Supervised	Mean Total Compensation	Median Total Compensation
1 - 2 People	$70,839	$72,000
3 - 4 People	$80,897	$75,000
5 - 6 People	$82,581	$75,000
7 - 8 People	$80,124	$77,000
9 - 10 People	$81,782	$70,500
11 - 15 People	$78,986	$79,000
16 - 20 People	$80,191	$75,000
21 - 25 People	$82,941	$75,000
26 - 50 People	$87,144	$82,500
51+ People	$123,829	$95,722

Total Compensation by Number of People in Project Management at Location

Number of People in Project Management at Location	Mean Total Compensation	Median Total Compensation
1 - 2 People	$79,549	$65,600
3 - 4 People	$70,970	$69,000
5 - 10 People	$83,173	$77,000
11 - 15 People	$85,413	$80,000
16 - 20 People	$79,370	$75,000
21 - 30 People	$78,212	$70,500
31+ People	$90,384	$79,100

Total Compensation by Number of People in Project Management in Organization

Number of People in Project Management in Organization	Mean Total Compensation	Median Total Compensation
1 - 10 People	$80,422	$71,000
11 - 25 People	$77,754	$78,735
26 - 50 People	$83,850	$72,500
51 - 100 People	$77,281	$76,000
101 - 300 People	$88,256	$77,250
300+ People	$75,433	$80,532

Executive Summary

Total Compensation by Number of Employees at Location

Number of Employees at Location	Mean Total Compensation	Median Total Compensation
1 - 10 People	$84,802	$76,500
11 - 20 People	$85,339	$73,500
21 - 50 People	$82,419	$70,500
51 - 100 People	$80,230	$76,000
101 - 200 People	$80,415	$75,000
201 - 500 People	$80,341	$71,547
501 - 1,000 People	$95,930	$77,250
1,001+ People	$78,984	$76,083

Total Compensation by Number of Employees in Organization

Number of Employees in Organization	Mean Total Compensation	Median Total Compensation
1 - 50 People	$91,595	$75,640
51 - 100 People	$73,528	$71,000
101 - 200 People	$80,992	$77,000
201 - 500 People	$77,382	$70,500
501 - 1,000 People	$79,704	$67,500
1,001 - 5,000 People	$79,807	$71,500
5,001 - 10,000 People	$79,787	$68,000
10,001 - 20,000 People	$84,762	$80,000
20,001+ People	$92,215	$80,000

Total Compensation by Number of Years in Project Management

Number of Years in Project Management	Mean Total Compensation	Median Total Compensation
1 - 2 Years	$65,508	$52,814
3 - 5 Years	$66,804	$65,000
6 - 10 Years	$81,228	$75,000
11 - 15 Years	$85,914	$80,000
16 - 20 Years	$98,150	$85,999
21+ Years	$112,005	$86,000

Total Compensation by Number of Years Worked for Current Employer

Number of Years Worked for Current Employer	Mean Total Compensation	Median Total Compensation
1 Year	$77,341	$74,113
2 Years	$77,354	$71,000
3 - 5 Years	$79,673	$70,000
6 - 10 Years	$78,298	$73,170
11 - 15 Years	$75,267	$98,500
16 - 20 Years	$89,383	$79,050
21+ Years	$101,455	$88,000

Executive Summary

Total Compensation by PMP Certification

PMP Certification	Mean Total Compensation	Median Total Compensation
PMP	$85,558	$80,000
Non PMP	$80,413	$71,000

Total Compensation by Gender

Gender	Mean Total Compensation	Median Total Compensation
Male	$85,174	$77,500
Female	$71,895	$68,718

Total Compensation by Age

Age	Mean Total Compensation	Median Total Compensation
25 - 34 Years	$62,493	$54,191
35 - 44 Years	$79,471	$75,000
45 - 54 Years	$92,152	$81,325
55 - 64 Years	$102,975	$88,000

Total Compensation by Education

Education	Mean Total Compensation	Median Total Compensation
High school degree or equivalent	$71,538	$61,917
Some college/AA degree or equivalent	$78,151	$70,000
College degree or equivalent	$76,549	$72,000
Master's degree or equivalent	$90,533	$79,000
Doctoral degree or equivalent	$93,610	$92,000

Executive Summary

Determinants of Total Compensation

The diagram on page 27 shows which personal and professional characteristics were most influential in determining respondents' total compensation. That is, the information contained in this diagram shows which characteristics perform best in predicting or explaining differences in respondents' total compensation. A chi-square automatic interaction detection (CHAID) analysis produced the information shown in the diagram on page 27.

On a global basis, job title/position was the number one determinant of total compensation for respondents. Respondents in upper-management positions* had the highest mean total compensation ($110,306), while respondents in management** earned $77,966 in mean total compensation.

Among respondents in upper management, number of years in project management was the best predictor of mean total compensation. Respondents in upper management with at least 16 years of experience in project management had a mean total compensation of $140,984 compared to their counterparts with 15 or fewer years of experience, whose mean total compensation was $93,327.

Mean project budget size was the final determinant of total compensation for respondents in upper management who had 15 or fewer years in project management. Respondents in upper management with 15 or fewer years in project management who were engaged in/managed projects with budgets greater than $2 million earned considerably more ($104,984) than their colleagues whose projects averaged less than $2 million ($83,915).

Total compensation for respondents in management was further explained by geographic location, respondents' age and PMP Certification. For example, respondents in management within the United States, Asia, or Europe earned considerably more in mean total compensation ($83,243) than their colleagues in other parts of the world ($62,146). Respondents in management within the United States, Asia, and Europe had their mean total compensation further explained by their age with those older than 35 earning $87,585 in mean total compensation and those less than 35 earning $64,093. Respondents in management who worked in Canada, Australia/New Zealand, the Middle East, and Latin America had their mean total compensation further explained by whether or not they had earned the PMP Certification. Respondents who had earned the PMP Certification averaged $72,390 in total compensation, while those who had not earned the PMP Certification averaged only $55,132.

The main determinant of mean total compensation for respondents who were project managers was geographic location with members working within the United States or Asia having a mean total compensation of $81,010 and their colleagues in other parts of the world having a mean total compensation of $44,202.

*Upper-management positions included CEO, CFO, CIO, etc., Senior Management, and Director of Project/Program Management.
**Management positions included Program Manager, Project Manager, and Project Management Consultant/Advisor.

Determinants of Global Compensation*

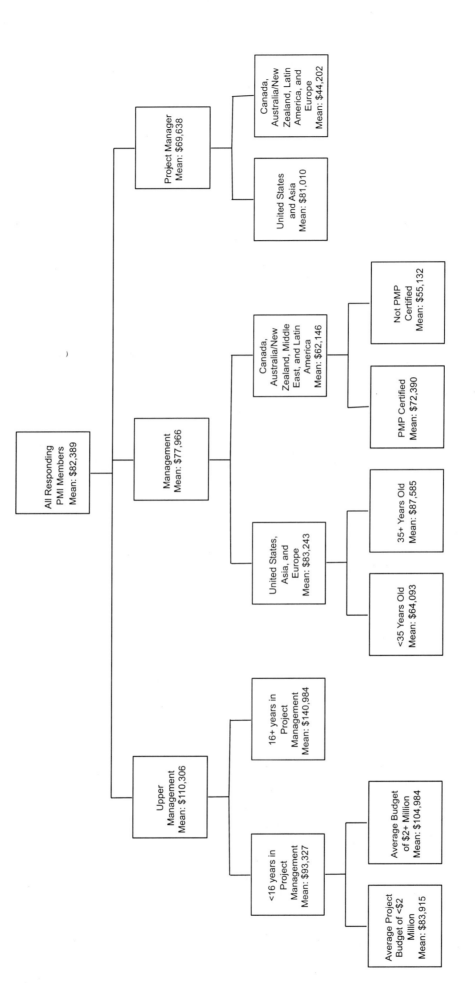

All Responding
PMI Members
Mean: $82,389

Project Manager
Mean: $69,638
- United States and Asia Mean: $81,010
- Canada, Australia/New Zealand, Latin America, and Europe Mean: $44,202

Management
Mean: $77,966
- United States, Asia, and Europe Mean: $83,243
  - <35 Years Old Mean: $64,093
  - 35+ Years Old Mean: $87,585
- Canada, Australia/New Zealand, Middle East, and Latin America Mean: $62,146
  - PMP Certified Mean: $72,390
  - Not PMP Certified Mean: $55,132

Upper Management
Mean: $110,306
- <16 years in Project Management Mean: $93,327
  - Average Project Budget of <$2 Million Mean: $83,915
  - Average Budget of $2+ Million Mean: $104,984
- 16+ years in Project Management Mean: $140,984

* Job title/position was the number one determinant of global compensation. That is, job title/position was the single best explanatory variable for global compensation. This chart was produced by CHAID analysis.

Executive Summary

Benefits

Insurance

%	Insurance
92%	Healthcare insurance
79%	Long-term disability insurance
72%	Short-term disability insurance
76%	Accidental death insurance
55%	Vision insurance
73%	Prescription drugs insurance
77%	Dental insurance
76%	Life insurance
15%	Professional liability insurance
	Insurance delivery/format
56%	Standard Plan
39%	Cafeteria Plan

Other Benefits

%	Other Benefits
76%	Retirement contributions by employer
47%	Performance incentive
8%	Retention incentive
10%	Signing bonus
30%	Stock options
20%	Relocation/travel bonus
13%	Holiday bonus
7%	Housing allowance/free housing
17%	Free participation in stock purchases
15%	Vehicle
10%	Entertainment allowance
18%	Club memberships
14%	Tickets to cultural events, sporting events, etc.
9%	At-risk bonus pay
4%	Mortgage paid by employer until house is sold
5%	Paid child care
38%	Maternity (paternity) leave
18%	Matched savings
4%	Sabbatical with pay
20%	Wellness program
55%	Free parking
4%	Adult dependent care
42%	Cellular telephone
58%	Laptop/home computer

Executive Summary

Mean Reimbursement Levels

%	Mean Reimbursement Levels
91%	Academic tuition
98%	Professional workshops
97%	Association dues

Retirement Plan

84% of respondents' employers offered retirement plans.

%	Retirement Plan
20%	Defined benefit
15%	Defined contribution
3%	IRA
1%	Money purchase plan
9%	401 (k)-type plan - employee only
46%	401 (k)-type plan - employer match
7%	Profit sharing
2%	Simplified employee plan
1%	Supplementary executive plan
1%	Tax sheltered annuity plan
10%	Employee stock options
6%	Flexible benefit plan

Vesting Period

%	Vesting Period
21%	No vesting period
79%	Vesting period
5%	6-month vesting period
11%	1-year vesting period
4%	2-year vesting period
32%	3–5-year vesting period
22%	>5-year vesting period

Paid Leave

Days	Paid Leave
19	Mean paid vacation days
17	Mean paid sick days
10	Mean paid holidays
11	Mean paid personal days

Executive Summary

PMP®Certification

36% of Respondents Earned PMP Certification

Support for Striving for PMP Certification

%	Support for Striving for PMP Certification
18%	Paid leave
65%	Pay for meetings/training
68%	Pay for examination application fee
57%	Employer recommends striving for PMP Certification
11%	Employer requires PMP Certification
17%	Employer rewards PMP Certification

Support for Maintaining PMP Certification

%	Support for Maintaining PMP Certification
15%	Paid leave
61%	Pay for meetings/training
58%	Employer recommends maintaining PMP Certification
10%	Employer requires maintaining PMP Certification
10%	Employer rewards maintaining PMP Certification

Respondent Profile

Employment

%	Employment
92%	Full-time employed
7%	Full-time self-employed
1%	Other

Hours Worked in a Typical Week

%	Hours Worked
25%	1 - 40 Hours
25%	41 - 45 Hours
31%	46 - 50 Hours
7%	51 - 55 Hours
9%	56 - 60 Hours
3%	61+ Hours

Executive Summary

Title within Organization

%	Title
3%	CEO, CFO, CIO, etc.
7%	Senior Management
8%	Director of Project/Program Management
1%	Professor/Academic
12%	Program Manager
40%	Project Manager
7%	Project Management Consultant/Advisor
2%	Project Engineer
5%	Project Team Leader
3%	Project Coordinator
2%	Project Planner/Scheduler
1%	Project Administrator
1%	Project Team Member
6%	Other

Executive Summary

Organization's Industry Affiliation

%	Organization's Industry Affiliation
Construction	
11%	Commercial/Heavy Industrial
3%	Residential
3%	Other Construction
Other Business Activities	
2%	Academia
3%	Aerospace
4%	Architectural Design
3%	Automation Services
10%	Business Management
19%	Computers/Software/DP
20%	Consulting
4%	Defense
13%	E-Business
2%	Economics/Finance
5%	Education/Training
4%	Environmental/Waste/Sewage
16%	Engineering
9%	Financial Services
4%	Health/Human/Social Services
28%	Information Technology
2%	International Development
1%	Legal
1%	Printing/Publishing
5%	Public Administration/Government
2%	Real Estate/Insurance
3%	Supply Chain
2%	Systems Security
17%	Telecommunications
4%	Transportation
1%	Urban Development
6%	Utilities

Executive Summary

Role within the Organization

%	*Role within the Organization*
Engineering	
4%	Civil
2%	Electrical
1%	Electronics
1%	Environment
1%	Industrial
3%	Mechanical
3%	Other Engineering
Management	
6%	Communications
3%	Configuration
9%	Contract/Procurement
8%	Corporate/Administrative
9%	Cost
2%	Critical Chain
5%	Earned Value
4%	Human Resources
16%	Information/Computer
2%	Materials
61%	Project/Program
8%	Quality
2%	Records
5%	Risk/Safety
3%	Site/Facility
15%	Time Management/Scheduling/Planning
Other	
16%	Consulting
1%	Finance
5%	Marketing/Business Development/Sales
1%	Production
3%	Project Accounting/Audit
3%	Research/Product Development
3%	Service & Outsourcing
5%	Teaching/Training
1%	Web Strategist/Technologist
2%	Other

Executive Summary

Responsibilities within the Organization (see page 11 for explanation)

%	Responsibilities within Organization
10%	Level 1
13%	Level 2
45%	Level 3
12%	Level 4
8%	Level 5
2%	Level 6
1%	Level 7
2%	Level 8
2%	Level 9
3%	Level 10
2%	Level 11

Geographic Scope of Projects Currently Engaged In/Managed

%	Geographic Scope
37%	Local
23%	State/Province
32%	Multi-State/Province
32%	Within One Country
24%	Multiple Countries
17%	Multiple Continents

Mean Budget Size of Typical Project Engaged In/Managed

%	Mean Budget Size
10%	<$100,000
10%	$100,000 - $249,999
10%	$250,000 - $499,999
10%	$500,000 - $999,999
10%	$1.0 - $1.99 Million
7%	$2.0 - $2.99 Million
5%	$3.0 - $3.99 Million
3%	$4.0 - $4.99 Million
9%	$5.0 - $9.99 Million
8%	$10.0 - $24.99 Million
5%	$25.0 - $49.99 Million
4%	$50.0 - $99.99 Million
6%	$100.0 - $499.99 Million
2%	$500.0 - $999.99 Million
1%	$1.0 - $9.99 Billion

Executive Summary

Current Number of Projects Engaged In/Managed

%	Current Number of Projects Engaged In/Managed
14%	1 Project
18%	2 Projects
20%	3 Projects
11%	4 Projects
9%	5 Projects
15%	6 - 10 Projects
13%	11+ Projects

Number of People Presently Supervised

%	Number of People Presently Supervised
7%	1 - 2 People Supervised
10%	3 - 4 People Supervised
12%	5 - 6 People Supervised
10%	7 - 8 People Supervised
11%	9 - 10 People Supervised
14%	11 - 15 People Supervised
10%	16 - 20 People Supervised
7%	21 - 25 People Supervised
10%	26 - 50 People Supervised
9%	51+ People Supervised

Number of People in Project/Program Management at Location

%	Number of People in Project/Program Management at Location
9%	1 - 2 People
12%	3 - 4 People
28%	5 - 10 People
10%	11 - 15 People
8%	16 - 20 People
10%	21 - 30 People
23%	31+ People

Number of People in Project/Program Management in Organization

%	Number of People in Project/Program Management in Organization
22%	1 - 10 People
14%	11 - 25 People
16%	26 - 50 People
14%	51 - 100 People
12%	101 - 300 People
22%	301+ People

Executive Summary

Number of Employees at Location

%	Number of Employees at Location
11%	1 - 10 People
7%	11 - 20 People
15%	21 - 50 People
14%	51 - 100 People
15%	101 - 200 People
16%	201 - 500 People
8%	501 - 1,000 People
14%	1,001+ People

Number of Employees in Entire Organization

%	Number of Employees in Organization
11%	1 - 50 People
6%	51 - 100 People
6%	101 - 200 People
14%	201 - 500 People
7%	501 - 1,000 People
22%	1,001 - 5,000 People
10%	5,001 - 10,000 People
7%	10,001 - 20,000 People
17%	20,001+ People

Total Years Worked in Project Management

%	Total Years Worked in Project Management
7%	1 - 2 Years
23%	3 - 5 Years
30%	6 - 10 Years
19%	11 - 15 Years
12%	16 - 20 Years
9%	21+ Years

Total Years Worked for Current Employer

%	Total Years Worked for Current Employer
17%	1 Year
12%	2 Years
21%	3 - 5 Years
15%	6 - 10 Years
11%	11 - 15 Years
10%	16 - 20 Years
14%	21+ Years

Executive Summary

Primary Work Environment

%	Primary Work Environment
84%	Traditional office
5%	Virtual office
6%	Home office
5%	Other

Other Workplace Issues

%	Other Workplace Issues
50%	Changed employers in past 5 years
31%	Relocated with same employer in past 5 years

Career Path

%	Career Path
23%	Career path clearly defined and in writing
45%	Informal or unstated career path
32%	No career path

Geographic Regions of Respondents

%		Geographic Regions
58%		United States
	22%	Northeast
	24%	Midwest
	24%	Southeast
	9%	Southwest
	7%	Plains/Mountain
	14%	Far West
15%		Canada
	13%	Alberta
	7%	British Columbia
	6%	Nova Scotia
	38%	Ontario
	21%	Quebec
	9%	Saskatchewan
	6%	Other
1%		Africa
8%		Asia
6%		Australia/New Zealand
2%		Middle East
4%		Latin America
6%		Europe

Executive Summary

Age of Respondents

%	Age of Respondents
1%	25 years of age or less
17%	25 - 34 years of age
41%	35 - 44 years of age
33%	45 - 54 years of age
7%	55 - 64 years of age
1%	65+ years of age

Education Level of Respondents

%	Education Level of Respondents
2%	High school degree
9%	Some college/AA degree
46%	College degree
39%	Master's degree
4%	Doctoral degree

Gender of Respondents

%	Gender of Respondents
75%	Male
25%	Female

Years as a PMI Member

%	Years as a PMI Member
44%	1 Year or less
19%	2 Years
13%	3 Years
6%	4 Years
7%	5 Years
8%	6 - 10 Years
3%	11+ Years

Compensation

Compensation by Geographic Area

This section of the report presents total compensation data for respondents by geographic location. Total compensation data are presented for all areas of the world for which there was sufficient information to present reliable and valid data. Total compensation information is also broken down by areas within the United States and some provinces of Canada. The following geographical areas are examined in this section of the report*:

United States
      Northeast
      Midwest
      Southeast
      Southwest
      Plains/Mountain
      Far West
Canada
      Alberta
      British Columbia
      Nova Scotia
      Ontario
      Quebec
      Saskatchewan
      Other
Asia
Australia/New Zealand
Europe
Latin America
Middle East

*See pages 5 through 6 for countries and areas included within each designation.

Tables on pages 43 through 51 show total compensation for respondents by geographic location. The global mean total compensation based on exchange rates was $82,389. Respondents in Asia ($111,883) and the United States ($87,807) exceeded this mean total compensation figure. The Asian figure is inflated by a few respondents who reported very high total compensation numbers. After removing these individuals from the analysis, Asian respondents' mean total compensation dropped to $90,075.

The mean total compensation for respondents in the United States was 7% greater than the global figure. Canada and Australia/New Zealand had mean total compensation figures that lagged behind the global average by 25% and 24%, respectively. These figures were significantly below the global mean.

Compensation by Geographic Area

A global view of mean total compensation for respondents based on Organisation for Economic Co-Operation & Development (OECD) purchasing power parities differed slightly from figures based on exchange rates (see page 43). Asia and the United States still had the highest values, (Asia's value is still inflated by a few respondents), while Canada had the lowest mean total compensation figure. However, when total compensation is based on the OECD's purchasing power parities, Canada and Australia/New Zealand exhibit relatively higher values. Canada's mean total compensation figure jumps from $61,614 (based on exchange rates) to $70,362 (based on purchasing power parities). Likewise, Australia/New Zealand experienced a jump in mean total compensation from $62,334 to $77,519 when moving from figures based on exchange rates to figures based on purchasing power parities. The United States was chosen as the "base" country because nearly 75% of PMI members work in the United States. Since the United States was the "base" country—i.e., exchange rates and purchasing power parities were pegged to United States data—figures for the United States remained the same regardless of whether mean total compensation was based on exchange rates or purchasing power parities.

Mean total compensation within the United States varied significantly with the western part of the country exhibiting the highest figure ($103,595). The Northeast had the second-highest figure ($90,158), but it was significantly below the mean total compensation reported by respondents from the Western United States. Respondents from the southwestern and southeastern parts of the United States reported the lowest mean total compensation figures.

Within Canada, mean total compensation did not vary significantly. Sample sizes were small within provinces so data within Canada should be interpreted cautiously.

Comparisons to 1996 [1]

In 1996, mean total compensation within the United States was $79,974 compared to $87,807 in 2000. The annual percentage increase in mean total compensation since 1996 was 2.4%. Respondents in Canada experienced a decrease in mean total compensation since 1996. Canadian respondents reported a mean total compensation figure of $74,258 in 1996, compared to $61,614 in 2000. Part of the decrease in Canadian respondents' mean total compensation in 2000 was a result of the Canadian dollar's fall in value vis-à-vis the United States dollar from 1996 to 2000.

Compensation by Geographic Area

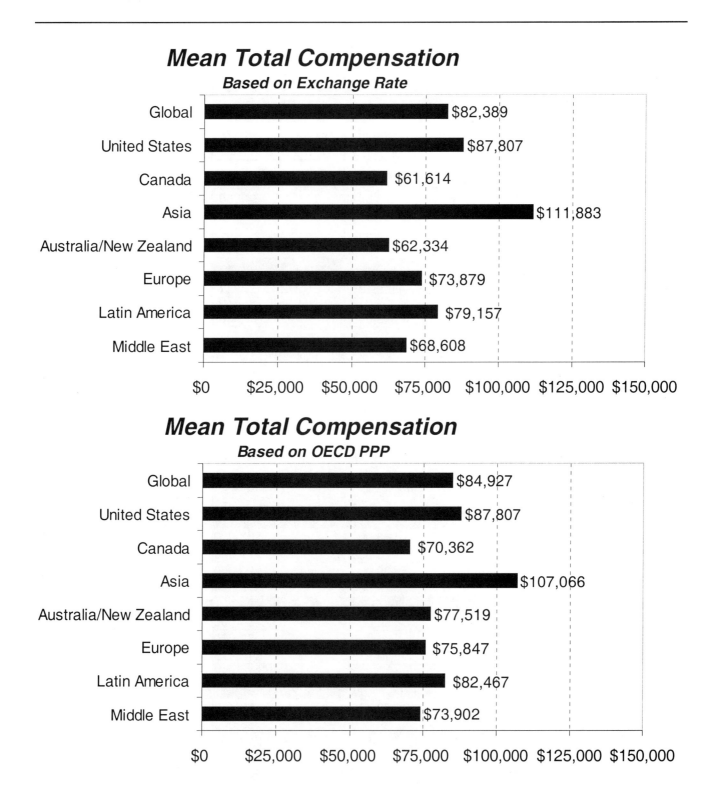

Mean Total Compensation
Based on Exchange Rate

Global	$82,389
United States	$87,807
Canada	$61,614
Asia	$111,883
Australia/New Zealand	$62,334
Europe	$73,879
Latin America	$79,157
Middle East	$68,608

Mean Total Compensation
Based on OECD PPP

Global	$84,927
United States	$87,807
Canada	$70,362
Asia	$107,066
Australia/New Zealand	$77,519
Europe	$75,847
Latin America	$82,467
Middle East	$73,902

Compensation by Geographic Area

Global

	Based on Exchange Rate	N	Based on OECD PPP	N
Salary		1,194		1,188
25th Percentile	$50,783		$55,556	
Median	$69,000		$70,000	
75th Percentile	$85,000		$86,975	
Mean	$73,243		$75,657	
Bonus		696		693
25th Percentile	$3,551		$4,000	
Median	$7,000		$7,500	
75th Percentile	$14,445		$15,000	
Mean	$13,000		$13,199	
Deferred Compensation		139		137
25th Percentile	$3,100		$3,300	
Median	$6,000		$6,870	
75th Percentile	$12,000		$13,000	
Mean	$13,959		$14,461	
Total Compensation		1,195		1,190
25th Percentile	$55,100		$60,000	
Median	$75,000		$76,000	
75th Percentile	$95,200		$96,500	
Mean	$82,389		$84,927	

United States

	Based on Exchange Rate	N	Based on OECD PPP	N
Salary		711		711
25th Percentile	$63,000		$63,000	
Median	$75,000		$75,000	
75th Percentile	$90,000		$90,000	
Mean	$79,504		$79,504	
Bonus		436		436
25th Percentile	$4,000		$4,000	
Median	$7,000		$7,000	
75th Percentile	$12,975		$12,975	
Mean	$10,927		$10,927	
Deferred Compensation		98		98
25th Percentile	$3,400		$3,400	
Median	$6,000		$6,000	
75th Percentile	$10,550		$10,550	
Mean	$12,414		$12,414	
Total Compensation		711		711
25th Percentile	$66,250		$66,250	
Median	$81,115		$81,115	
75th Percentile	$98,850		$98,850	
Mean	$87,807		$87,807	

Compensation by Geographic Area

Canada

	Based on Exchange Rate	N	Based on OECD PPP	N
Salary		167		167
25th Percentile	$40,626		$50,000	
Median	$50,000		$58,974	
75th Percentile	$60,000		$72,068	
Mean	$55,542		$63,215	
Bonus		98		98
25th Percentile	$2,708		$3,419	
Median	$4,740		$5,614	
75th Percentile	$10,000		$10,256	
Mean	$7,771		$9,359	
Deferred Compensation		13		13
25th Percentile	$2,016		$2,282	
Median	$4,063		$5,128	
75th Percentile	$33,178		$40,385	
Mean	$19,424		$21,268	
Total Compensation		167		167
25th Percentile	$44,000		$50,405	
Median	$52,814		$64,103	
75th Percentile	$63,647		$75,214	
Mean	$61,614		$70,362	

Asia

	Based on Exchange Rate	N	Based on OECD PPP	N
Salary		84		84
25th Percentile	$49,357		$47,127	
Median	$75,640		$65,500	
75th Percentile	$94,062		$85,536	
Mean	$81,242		$77,364	
Bonus		55		55
25th Percentile	$8,000		$8,197	
Median	$18,910		$18,634	
75th Percentile	$33,272		$30,000	
Mean	$41,568		$39,952	
Deferred Compensation		--		--
25th Percentile	--		--	
Median	--		--	
75th Percentile	--		--	
Mean	--		--	
Total Compensation		84		84
25th Percentile	$62,125		$57,094	
Median	$93,025		$80,000	
75th Percentile	$119,059		$106,000	
Mean	$111,883		$107,066	

Compensation by Geographic Area

Australia/New Zealand

	Based on Exchange Rate	N	Based on OECD PPP	N
Salary		71		71
25th Percentile	$40,000		$49,618	
Median	$49,997		$59,121	
75th Percentile	$63,000		$78,626	
Mean	$58,336		$72,647	
Bonus		29		29
25th Percentile	$2,720		$3,158	
Median	$5,000		$6,081	
75th Percentile	$13,235		$17,176	
Mean	$8,985		$11,072	
Deferred Compensation	--		--	
25th Percentile	--		--	
Median	--		--	
75th Percentile	--		--	
Mean	--		--	
Total Compensation		71		71
25th Percentile	$40,000		$50,000	
Median	$50,000		$63,000	
75th Percentile	$70,000		$88,000	
Mean	$62,334		$77,519	

Europe

	Based on Exchange Rate	N	Based on OECD PPP	N
Salary		74		74
25th Percentile	$42,423		$42,273	
Median	$59,586		$61,278	
75th Percentile	$90,435		$92,771	
Mean	$67,100		$69,008	
Bonus		39		39
25th Percentile	$2,200		$2,250	
Median	$5,000		$5,000	
75th Percentile	$15,000		$15,385	
Mean	$12,207		$12,303	
Deferred Compensation	--		--	
25th Percentile	--		--	
Median	--		--	
75th Percentile	--		--	
Mean	--		--	
Total Compensation		74		74
25th Percentile	$43,054		$46,554	
Median	$66,529		$70,000	
75th Percentile	$95,490		$100,000	
Mean	$73,879		$75,847	

Compensation by Geographic Area

Latin America

	Based on Exchange Rate	N	Based on OECD PPP	N
Salary		49		49
25th Percentile	$30,000		$31,371	
Median	$54,000		$54,000	
75th Percentile	$75,000		$77,500	
Mean	$70,633		$73,317	
Bonus		22		22
25th Percentile	$3,533		$4,650	
Median	$8,334		$9,500	
75th Percentile	$21,000		$21,000	
Mean	$15,422		$16,703	
Deferred Compensation		--		--
25th Percentile	--		--	
Median	--		--	
75th Percentile	--		--	
Mean	--		--	
Total Compensation		49		49
25th Percentile	$34,696		$36,500	
Median	$62,517		$65,000	
75th Percentile	$83,000		$86,400	
Mean	$79,157		$82,467	

Middle East

	Based on Exchange Rate	N	Based on OECD PPP	N
Salary		28		23
25th Percentile	$26,945		$40,000	
Median	$57,500		$60,000	
75th Percentile	$82,949		$96,000	
Mean	$61,454		$66,467	
Bonus		13		--
25th Percentile	$4,288		--	
Median	$6,536		--	
75th Percentile	$18,675		--	
Mean	$10,939		--	
Deferred Compensation		--		--
25th Percentile	--		--	
Median	--		--	
75th Percentile	--		--	
Mean	--		--	
Total Compensation		28		23
25th Percentile	$38,438		$41,700	
Median	$62,500		$66,000	
75th Percentile	$96,294		$98,000	
Mean	$68,608		$73,902	

Compensation by United States Regions

Northeast

	Based on Exchange Rate	N	Based on OECD PPP	N
Salary		147		147
25th Percentile	$70,000		$70,000	
Median	$80,000		$80,000	
75th Percentile	$90,500		$90,500	
Mean	$82,728		$82,728	
Bonus		96		96
25th Percentile	$4,500		$4,500	
Median	$7,450		$7,450	
75th Percentile	$12,000		$12,000	
Mean	$10,029		$10,029	
Deferred Compensation		17		17
25th Percentile	$3,750		$3,750	
Median	$10,000		$10,000	
75th Percentile	$12,000		$12,000	
Mean	$12,709		$12,709	
Total Compensation		148		148
25th Percentile	$72,000		$72,000	
Median	$85,500		$85,500	
75th Percentile	$105,000		$105,000	
Mean	$90,158		$90,158	

Midwest

	Based on Exchange Rate	N	Based on OECD PPP	N
Salary		176		176
25th Percentile	$60,250		$60,250	
Median	$72,000		$72,000	
75th Percentile	$85,000		$85,000	
Mean	$75,258		$75,258	
Bonus		115		115
25th Percentile	$4,000		$4,000	
Median	$7,600		$7,600	
75th Percentile	$14,000		$14,000	
Mean	$11,434		$11,434	
Deferred Compensation		29		29
25th Percentile	$3,000		$3,000	
Median	$6,000		$6,000	
75th Percentile	$10,000		$10,000	
Mean	$9,497		$9,497	
Total Compensation		176		176
25th Percentile	$64,625		$64,625	
Median	$80,000		$80,000	
75th Percentile	$95,750		$95,750	
Mean	$84,299		$84,299	

Compensation by United States Regions

Southeast

	Based on Exchange Rate	N	Based on OECD PPP	N
Salary		171		171
25th Percentile	$62,000		$62,000	
Median	$73,000		$73,000	
75th Percentile	$90,000		$90,000	
Mean	$75,792		$75,792	
Bonus		103		103
25th Percentile	$4,000		$4,000	
Median	$7,000		$7,000	
75th Percentile	$12,000		$12,000	
Mean	$8,650		$8,650	
Deferred Compensation		17		17
25th Percentile	$3,545		$3,545	
Median	$4,000		$4,000	
75th Percentile	$10,350		$10,350	
Mean	$9,331		$9,331	
Total Compensation		171		171
25th Percentile	$65,600		$65,600	
Median	$78,000		$78,000	
75th Percentile	$95,000		$95,000	
Mean	$81,960		$81,960	

Southwest

	Based on Exchange Rate	N	Based on OECD PPP	N
Salary		65		65
25th Percentile	$64,400		$64,400	
Median	$71,000		$71,000	
75th Percentile	$85,000		$85,000	
Mean	$75,579		$75,579	
Bonus		43		43
25th Percentile	$4,000		$4,000	
Median	$6,000		$6,000	
75th Percentile	$10,000		$10,000	
Mean	$7,581		$7,581	
Deferred Compensation		13		13
25th Percentile	$2,250		$2,250	
Median	$5,000		$5,000	
75th Percentile	$10,000		$10,000	
Mean	$6,963		$6,963	
Total Compensation		65		65
25th Percentile	$65,200		$65,200	
Median	$77,000		$77,000	
75th Percentile	$93,450		$93,450	
Mean	$81,987		$81,987	

Compensation by United States Regions

Plains/Mountain

	Based on Exchange Rate	N	Based on OECD PPP	N
Salary		48		48
25th Percentile	$65,625		$65,625	
Median	$76,500		$76,500	
75th Percentile	$99,250		$99,250	
Mean	$81,870		$81,870	
Bonus		25		25
25th Percentile	$4,100		$4,100	
Median	$7,000		$7,000	
75th Percentile	$17,000		$17,000	
Mean	$10,783		$10,783	
Deferred Compensation		--		--
25th Percentile	--		--	
Median	--		--	
75th Percentile	--		--	
Mean	--		--	
Total Compensation		48		48
25th Percentile	$68,000		$68,000	
Median	$81,125		$81,125	
75th Percentile	$109,950		$109,950	
Mean	$88,507		$88,507	

Far West

	Based on Exchange Rate	N	Based on OECD PPP	N
Salary		99		99
25th Percentile	$60,000		$60,000	
Median	$80,000		$80,000	
75th Percentile	$92,000		$92,000	
Mean	$90,103		$90,103	
Bonus		51		51
25th Percentile	$4,000		$4,000	
Median	$10,000		$10,000	
75th Percentile	$18,000		$18,000	
Mean	$17,804		$17,804	
Deferred Compensation		19		19
25th Percentile	$4,800		$4,800	
Median	$8,000		$8,000	
75th Percentile	$15,000		$15,000	
Mean	$22,472		$22,472	
Total Compensation		99		99
25th Percentile	$63,000		$63,000	
Median	$83,000		$83,000	
75th Percentile	$103,000		$103,000	
Mean	$103,595		$103,595	

Compensation by Canadian Provinces

Canada

Total Compensation Based on Exchange Rate

	N	25th Percentile	Median	75th Percentile	Mean
Alberta	23	$39,408	$52,814	$59,585	$61,184
British Columbia	12	$45,839	$49,801	$61,108	$56,621
Nova Scotia	10	$37,240	$46,043	$51,290	$66,535
Ontario	64	$46,381	$56,876	$68,500	$61,343
Quebec	33	$34,701	$51,676	$57,824	$61,254
Saskatchewan	14	$43,790	$54,845	$83,684	$62,245
Other	10	$41,642	$53,000	$67,033	$65,986

Total Compensation Based on OECD PPP

	N	25th Percentile	Median	75th Percentile	Mean
Alberta	23	$49,743	$64,103	$75,214	$72,675
British Columbia	12	$57,031	$62,863	$71,896	$66,379
Nova Scotia	10	$47,008	$58,119	$64,743	$76,773
Ontario	64	$55,556	$66,324	$76,692	$71,678
Quebec	33	$41,880	$52,520	$72,991	$62,185
Saskatchewan	14	$48,487	$69,231	$93,247	$72,059
Other	10	$50,962	$53,000	$84,615	$79,192

Compensation by Employment Status

Information was examined for respondents who were full-time employed by an organization versus those who were full-time self-employed (see page 53). Respondents who were self-employed had considerably higher mean total compensation ($109,122) than individuals who were full-time employed by other organizations ($81,104). As shown later in the report, individuals who were full-time employed by organizations had better benefit packages than individuals who were full-time self-employed.

The reader should note that there were relatively few respondents (64) who reported being full-time self-employed. Because of the paucity of full-time self-employed respondents, comparisons were made only on a global, United States, and Canada basis. Data were consistent across these three geographic areas with full-time, self-employed respondents having significantly higher mean total compensation. Full-time, self-employed individuals in the United States reported the highest mean total compensation ($131,652), yet there were only 23 respondents in this category.

Compensation by Employment Status

Global

Total Compensation Based on Exchange Rate

	N	25th Percentile	Median	75th Percentile	Mean
Full-time employed	1,101	$55,311	$74,482	$95,000	$81,104
Full-time self-employed	64	$60,235	$92,000	$138,750	$109,122

Total Compensation Based on OECD PPP

	N	25th Percentile	Median	75th Percentile	Mean
Full-time employed	1,096	$60,000	$75,000	$95,000	$83,209
Full-time self-employed	64	$72,163	$100,000	$149,882	$119,819

United States

Total Compensation Based on Exchange Rate

	N	25th Percentile	Median	75th Percentile	Mean
Full-time employed	671	$66,000	$80,500	$97,600	$86,304
Full-time self-employed	23	$85,000	$130,000	$170,000	$131,652

Total Compensation Based on OECD PPP

	N	25th Percentile	Median	75th Percentile	Mean
Full-time employed	671	$66,000	$80,500	$97,600	$86,304
Full-time self-employed	23	$85,000	$130,000	$170,000	$131,652

Canada

Total Compensation Based on Exchange Rate

	N	25th Percentile	Median	75th Percentile	Mean
Full-time employed	152	$44,012	$52,460	$62,030	$58,568
Full-time self-employed	12	$44,858	$82,580	$174,223	$111,880

Total Compensation Based on OECD PPP

	N	25th Percentile	Median	75th Percentile	Mean
Full-time employed	152	$50,570	$64,000	$74,269	$67,113
Full-time self-employed	12	$56,624	$92,436	$219,433	$124,501

Compensation by Hours Worked

Hours worked were directly correlated with mean total compensation except for the highest category of number of hours worked (see page 55). Respondents working less than 40 hours a week had a mean total compensation of $71,475, while those working more than 55 hours a week had a mean total compensation that exceeded $100,000.

The relationship between hours worked and mean total compensation was more pronounced in the United States with individuals working less than 40 hours a week reporting $80,732 as their mean total compensation and respondents working over 60 hours a week reporting $109,600 as their mean total compensation.

Relatively few respondents per region limited the degree of analysis of mean total compensation by hours worked by country. For other regions, mean total compensation was examined for those who worked 40 or fewer hours versus those who worked more than 40 hours. In some regions, the difference in mean total compensation between those who labored long hours and those whose workweeks were shorter was minimal (e.g., Canada where there was a differential of approximately $4,500), while the difference was quite large in other countries (e.g., Asia where the difference was $57,000, and Latin America where the difference was $38,000). Yet, for all regions examined, there was a definite increase in mean total compensation based on hours worked per week.

Compensation by Hours Worked

Global

Total Compensation Based on Exchange Rate

	N	25th Percentile	Median	75th Percentile	Mean
1 - 40 Hours	290	$45,366	$63,250	$86,000	$71,475
41 - 45 Hours	292	$54,042	$72,797	$87,000	$75,680
46 - 50 Hours	348	$60,146	$80,000	$100,000	$89,061
51 - 55 Hours	80	$60,200	$80,000	$103,500	$82,474
56 - 60 Hours	103	$64,500	$85,999	$110,000	$105,269
61+ Hours	25	$60,502	$88,682	$119,300	$103,110

Total Compensation Based on OECD PPP

	N	25th Percentile	Median	75th Percentile	Mean
1 - 40 Hours	289	$51,282	$68,323	$85,500	$74,947
41 - 45 Hours	291	$58,200	$75,000	$89,800	$77,276
46 - 50 Hours	346	$65,000	$80,000	$101,743	$91,395
51 - 55 Hours	80	$65,000	$80,000	$104,750	$83,996
56 - 60 Hours	102	$66,725	$89,250	$110,000	$108,338
61+ Hours	25	$70,000	$91,000	$125,000	$108,502

United States

Total Compensation Based on Exchange Rate

	N	25th Percentile	Median	75th Percentile	Mean
1 - 40 Hours	134	$60,750	$73,146	$88,850	$80,732
41 - 45 Hours	188	$65,000	$80,000	$91,875	$82,449
46 - 50 Hours	233	$69,000	$83,600	$100,500	$91,047
51 - 55 Hours	53	$68,000	$91,000	$105,500	$89,634
56 - 60 Hours	59	$72,500	$95,000	$118,000	$102,275
61+ Hours	11	$68,000	$85,000	$127,000	$109,600

Total Compensation Based on OECD PPP

	N	25th Percentile	Median	75th Percentile	Mean
1 - 40 Hours	134	$60,750	$73,146	$88,850	$80,732
41 - 45 Hours	188	$65,000	$80,000	$91,875	$82,449
46 - 50 Hours	233	$69,000	$83,600	$100,500	$91,047
51 - 55 Hours	53	$68,000	$91,000	$105,500	$89,634
56 - 60 Hours	59	$72,500	$95,000	$118,000	$102,275
61+ Hours	11	$68,000	$85,000	$127,000	$109,600

Compensation by Hours Worked

Canada

Total Compensation Based on Exchange Rate

	N	25th Percentile	Median	75th Percentile	Mean
1 - 40 Hours	68	$38,395	$50,222	$60,197	$59,142
41+ Hours	95	$46,600	$54,169	$72,300	$63,630

Total Compensation Based on OECD PPP

	N	25th Percentile	Median	75th Percentile	Mean
1 - 40 Hours	68	$47,223	$59,829	$73,932	$69,889
41+ Hours	95	$51,282	$66,667	$76,923	$70,699

Asia

Total Compensation Based on Exchange Rate

	N	25th Percentile	Median	75th Percentile	Mean
1 - 40 Hours	38	$60,750	$83,157	$104,005	$80,243
41+ Hours	45	$63,447	$100,000	$130,000	$137,309

Total Compensation Based on OECD PPP

	N	25th Percentile	Median	75th Percentile	Mean
1 - 40 Hours	38	$55,354	$74,534	$96,250	$75,181
41+ Hours	45	$60,711	$88,000	$125,000	$132,593

Australia/New Zealand

Total Compensation Based on Exchange Rate

	N	25th Percentile	Median	75th Percentile	Mean
1 - 40 Hours	14	$35,090	$46,729	$55,198	$46,967
41+ Hours	49	$40,000	$50,000	$75,562	$65,130

Total Compensation Based on OECD PPP

	N	25th Percentile	Median	75th Percentile	Mean
1 - 40 Hours	14	$44,352	$63,524	$71,660	$61,877
41+ Hours	49	$50,000	$60,811	$87,515	$80,166

Compensation by Hours Worked

Europe

Total Compensation Based on Exchange Rate

	N	25th Percentile	Median	75th Percentile	Mean
1 - 40 Hours	13	$35,379	$47,200	$56,785	$63,397
41+ Hours	57	$54,473	$70,000	$101,604	$79,012

Total Compensation Based on OECD PPP

	N	25th Percentile	Median	75th Percentile	Mean
1 - 40 Hours	13	$41,208	$50,000	$88,311	$75,478
41+ Hours	57	$51,678	$70,000	$100,829	$78,767

Latin America

Total Compensation Based on Exchange Rate

	N	25th Percentile	Median	75th Percentile	Mean
1 - 40 Hours	14	$34,293	$39,300	$89,850	$54,151
41+ Hours	31	$30,000	$70,000	$85,000	$92,535

Total Compensation Based on OECD PPP

	N	25th Percentile	Median	75th Percentile	Mean
1 - 40 Hours	14	$35,125	$44,300	$89,850	$58,133
41+ Hours	31	$35,000	$70,000	$96,000	$95,968

Middle East

Total Compensation Based on Exchange Rate

	N	25th Percentile	Median	75th Percentile	Mean
1 - 40 Hours	--	--	--	--	--
41+ Hours	21	$29,604	$50,000	$81,730	$58,246

Total Compensation Based on OECD PPP

	N	25th Percentile	Median	75th Percentile	Mean
1 - 40 Hours	--	--	--	--	--
41+ Hours	17	$38,959	$60,000	$91,222	$64,574

Compensation by Title

Job title had a major impact on mean total compensation as data on pages 59 through 63 demonstrate. World-wide, CEOs, CFOs, CIOs, etc., reported a mean total compensation of $134,195. Senior management had a mean total compensation of $117,935. Number of respondents limited analysis of mean total compensation by several job titles. Tables on page 59 show global figures based on exchange rates and based on OECD purchasing power parities for several job titles.

Analyses of mean total compensation by job title by geographic area are shown on pages 60 through 63. Because of sample sizes, job titles were condensed into four levels where necessary:

Upper Management
> CEO, CFO, CIO, etc., Senior Management, and Director of Project/Program Management

Management
> Program Manager, Project Manager, and Project Management Consultant/Advisor

Project Member
> Project Engineer, Project Team Leader, Project Coordinator, Project Planner/Scheduler, Project Administrator, and Project Team Member

Other
> Professor/Academic, Researcher, Trainer, and Other

Comparisons to 1996 [1]

Comparisons to 1996 data are available only for the United States and are shown below. Figures are based on *median* rather than *mean* data to reduce the impact of extreme values on small sample sizes.

Median Total Compensation

	1996	2000	Annual % Increase (Decrease)
CEO, CFO, CIO, etc.	$99,500	$142,500	10.8%
Senior Management	$100,000	$98,000	(0.5%)
Director of Project/Program Management	$83,000	$100,000	5.1%
Program Manager	$75,000	$90,839	5.3%
Project Manager	$66,000	$77,000	4.2%
Project Management/Consultant/Advisor	$70,000	$85,000	5.4%
Project Engineer	$60,000	$70,200	4.3%
Project Team Leader	$58,620	$72,500	5.9%
Project Coordinator	$50,200	$58,500	4.1%
Project Planner/Scheduler	$56,500	$71,300	6.6%

Compensation by Title

Global
Total Compensation Based on Exchange Rate

	N	25th Percentile	Median	75th Percentile	Mean
CEO, CFO, CIO, etc.	36	$60,365	$98,780	$159,000	$134,195
Senior Management	86	$64,200	$90,000	$120,000	$117,935
Director of Project/Program Management	98	$74,325	$94,000	$120,000	$97,080
Professor/Academic	--	--	--	--	--
Program Manager	151	$65,666	$86,000	$105,000	$88,465
Project Manager	478	$52,907	$68,715	$86,125	$73,648
Project Management Consultant/Advisor	87	$60,939	$79,422	$96,149	$83,544
Project Engineer	28	$46,274	$61,500	$74,825	$60,570
Project Team Leader	55	$41,980	$66,185	$77,500	$64,192
Project Coordinator	31	$30,000	$47,000	$73,510	$55,908
Project Planner/Scheduler	19	$51,000	$74,100	$84,638	$65,872
Project Administrator	--	--	--	--	--
Project Team Member	15	$44,012	$58,600	$80,000	$125,236
Researcher	--	--	--	--	--
Trainer	--	--	--	--	--

Global
Total Compensation Based on OECD PPP

	N	25th Percentile	Median	75th Percentile	Mean
CEO, CFO, CIO, etc.	36	$70,500	$100,500	$171,080	$140,410
Senior Management	86	$71,346	$92,200	$120,000	$120,445
Director of Project/Program Management	98	$77,360	$94,500	$122,250	$99,671
Professor/Academic	--	--	--	--	--
Program Manager	151	$70,000	$88,000	$106,000	$91,278
Project Manager	477	$57,350	$70,086	$86,950	$75,529
Project Management Consultant/Advisor	86	$64,971	$79,600	$98,500	$86,299
Project Engineer	28	$50,556	$61,500	$73,887	$63,752
Project Team Leader	55	$50,341	$68,323	$76,083	$65,592
Project Coordinator	31	$36,752	$57,000	$72,000	$59,446
Project Planner/Scheduler	19	$54,000	$74,100	$85,000	$69,915
Project Administrator	--	--	--	--	--
Project Team Member	15	$53,417	$62,675	$100,225	$133,868
Researcher	--	--	--	--	--
Trainer	--	--	--	--	--

Compensation by Title

United States
Total Compensation Based on Exchange Rate

	N	25th Percentile	Median	75th Percentile	Mean
CEO, CFO, CIO, etc.	12	$105,000	$142,500	$296,250	$217,500
Senior Management	39	$83,600	$98,000	$130,000	$113,173
Director of Project/Program Management	57	$85,200	$100,000	$124,000	$104,102
Professor/Academic	--	--	--	--	--
Program Manager	108	$71,000	$90,839	$106,000	$92,358
Project Manager	299	$63,527	$77,000	$88,000	$77,684
Project Management Consultant/Advisor	43	$70,500	$85,000	$110,000	$99,458
Project Engineer	13	$59,100	$70,200	$73,500	$68,185
Project Team Leader	34	$61,550	$72,500	$82,750	$73,160
Project Coordinator	18	$42,375	$58,500	$91,125	$63,767
Project Planner/Scheduler	12	$54,250	$71,300	$83,750	$69,008
Project Administrator	--	--	--	--	--
Project Team Member	--	--	--	--	--
Researcher	--	--	--	--	--
Trainer	--	--	--	--	--

United States
Total Compensation Based on OECD PPP

	N	25th Percentile	Median	75th Percentile	Mean
CEO, CFO, CIO, etc.	12	$105,000	$142,500	$296,250	$217,500
Senior Management	39	$83,600	$98,000	$130,000	$113,173
Director of Project/Program Management	57	$85,200	$100,000	$124,000	$104,102
Professor/Academic	--	--	--	--	--
Program Manager	108	$71,000	$90,839	$106,000	$92,358
Project Manager	299	$63,527	$77,000	$88,000	$77,684
Project Management Consultant/Advisor	43	$70,500	$85,000	$110,000	$99,458
Project Engineer	13	$59,100	$70,200	$73,500	$68,185
Project Team Leader	34	$61,550	$72,500	$82,750	$73,160
Project Coordinator	18	$42,375	$58,500	$91,125	$63,767
Project Planner/Scheduler	12	$54,250	$71,300	$83,750	$69,008
Project Administrator	--	--	--	--	--
Project Team Member	--	--	--	--	--
Researcher	--	--	--	--	--
Trainer	--	--	--	--	--

Compensation by Title

Canada

Total Compensation Based on Exchange Rate

	N	25th Percentile	Median	75th Percentile	Mean
Upper Management	33	$51,591	$59,585	$95,500	$79,195
Management	100	$44,164	$52,396	$62,030	$61,225
Project Member	27	$35,209	$44,011	$54,160	$41,639
Other	--	--	--	--	--

Total Compensation Based on OECD PPP

	N	25th Percentile	Median	75th Percentile	Mean
Upper Management	33	$53,500	$72,650	$103,491	$88,255
Management	100	$51,070	$65,521	$75,214	$69,450
Project Member	27	$44,445	$53,000	$67,949	$56,301
Other	--	--	--	--	--

Asia

Total Compensation Based on Exchange Rate

	N	25th Percentile	Median	75th Percentile	Mean
Upper Management	18	$60,875	$105,000	$135,679	$179,825
Management	42	$58,544	$93,525	$123,500	$90,619
Project Member	16	$58,250	$80,000	$101,928	$72,974
Other	--	--	--	--	--

Total Compensation Based on OECD PPP

	N	25th Percentile	Median	75th Percentile	Mean
Upper Management	18	$60,875	$96,689	$126,250	$176,670
Management	42	$56,231	$78,479	$110,867	$85,664
Project Member	16	$50,660	$68,323	$78,750	$65,167
Other	--	--	--	--	--

Compensation by Title

Australia/New Zealand

Total Compensation Based on Exchange Rate

	N	25th Percentile	Median	75th Percentile	Mean
Upper Management	12	$52,205	$84,867	$99,263	$81,355
Management	48	$40,449	$50,300	$67,879	$63,078
Project Member	--	--	--	--	--
Other	--	--	--	--	--

Total Compensation Based on OECD PPP

	N	25th Percentile	Median	75th Percentile	Mean
Upper Management	12	$69,246	$109,160	$124,871	$100,589
Management	48	$50,150	$62,581	$80,401	$77,579
Project Member	--	--	--	--	--
Other	--	--	--	--	--

Europe

Total Compensation Based on Exchange Rate

	N	25th Percentile	Median	75th Percentile	Mean
Upper Management	21	$42,750	$86,000	$107,500	$81,252
Management	42	$52,634	$69,500	$87,210	$77,725
Project Member	--	--	--	--	--
Other	--	--	--	--	--

Total Compensation Based on OECD PPP

	N	25th Percentile	Median	75th Percentile	Mean
Upper Management	21	$41,250	$90,361	$108,050	$80,854
Management	42	$52,600	$70,000	$87,349	$78,527
Project Member	--	--	--	--	--
Other	--	--	--	--	--

Compensation by Title

Latin America

Total Compensation Based on Exchange Rate

	N	25th Percentile	Median	75th Percentile	Mean
Upper Management	15	$65,000	$80,000	$100,000	$131,733
Management	21	$32,196	$58,000	$86,400	$62,452
Project Member	--	--	--	--	--
Other	--	--	--	--	--

Total Compensation Based on OECD PPP

	N	25th Percentile	Median	75th Percentile	Mean
Upper Management	15	$65,000	$80,000	$100,000	$131,733
Management	21	$36,250	$58,000	$91,900	$67,967
Project Member	--	--	--	--	--
Other	--	--	--	--	--

Middle East

Total Compensation Based on Exchange Rate

	N	25th Percentile	Median	75th Percentile	Mean
Upper Management	11	$60,000	$86,000	$100,000	$84,579
Management	--	--	--	--	--
Project Member	--	--	--	--	--
Other	--	--	--	--	--

Total Compensation Based on OECD PPP

	N	25th Percentile	Median	75th Percentile	Mean
Upper Management	11	$60,000	$86,000	$100,000	$84,579
Management	--	--	--	--	--
Project Member	--	--	--	--	--
Other	--	--	--	--	--

Compensation by Industry Affiliation

Fifty-three (53) industry affiliations were listed on the survey. Sufficient responses were received to analyze mean total global compensation for 40 of these industry affiliations. Mean total compensation for these 40 industries are shown on pages 65 through 68. Industries that had the highest levels of mean total compensation were:

$111,802	Electrical/Electronic
$104,967	International Development
$103,733	Web Technology
$101,290	Chemical
$101,192	Utilities

Conversely, industries that had the lowest mean total compensations were:

$66,373	Automation Services
$67,318	Academia
$68,512	Health/Human/Social Services
$69,646	Other Business Activities
$70,360	Public Administration/Government

Compensation by Industry Affiliation

Global
Total Compensation Based on Exchange Rate

	N	25th Percentile	Median	75th Percentile	Mean
Construction					
Commercial/Heavy Industrial	129	$55,761	$80,000	$100,000	$84,033
Residential	29	$41,901	$61,893	$91,000	$71,479
Other Construction	36	$54,153	$78,500	$97,500	$77,261
Other Business Activities					
Academia	23	$31,300	$49,000	$95,000	$67,318
Aerospace	32	$61,088	$84,000	$101,000	$84,618
Architecture/Design	50	$47,965	$63,758	$95,125	$75,565
Arts/Entertainment/Broadcasting	--	--	--	--	--
Automation Services	39	$49,429	$59,594	$82,000	$66,373
Business Management	120	$57,554	$77,500	$110,000	$91,576
City Management	--	--	--	--	--
Computers/Software/DP	225	$62,258	$81,000	$101,500	$89,039
Consulting	237	$59,797	$82,000	$106,000	$92,371
Defense	46	$55,000	$71,500	$90,874	$73,004
E-Business	151	$59,505	$77,000	$105,000	$92,665
Economics/Finance	17	$63,449	$75,000	$126,800	$94,981
Education/Training	54	$59,750	$80,000	$114,000	$86,488
Environmental/Waste/Sewage	48	$54,750	$80,184	$98,750	$81,865
Engineering	185	$58,000	$79,460	$95,000	$84,244
Financial Services	101	$59,750	$74,000	$91,500	$78,315
Health/Human/Social Services	39	$39,949	$60,000	$90,000	$68,512
Information Technology	341	$57,277	$75,000	$93,250	$87,339
International Development	24	$69,250	$93,000	$119,250	$104,967
Legal	--	--	--	--	--
Printing/Publishing	--	--	--	--	--
Public Administration/Government	63	$50,783	$65,000	$82,000	$70,360
Real Estate/Insurance	20	$53,757	$73,250	$93,250	$74,680
Recreation	--	--	--	--	--
Supply Chain	37	$59,797	$80,000	$107,388	$88,469
Systems Security	27	$52,238	$69,000	$90,000	$75,995
Telecommunications	200	$51,155	$71,547	$93,975	$75,898
Transportation	49	$60,568	$81,500	$100,750	$87,201
Urban Development	14	$49,074	$78,425	$111,750	$86,582
Utilities	66	$59,427	$80,934	$109,138	$101,192

Compensation by Industry Affiliation

Global
Total Compensation Based on Exchange Rate

	N	25th Percentile	Median	75th Percentile	Mean
Other Business Activities (cont.)					
Web Technology	113	$61,469	$79,460	$105,500	$103,733
Other Business Activities	80	$42,837	$66,734	$86,500	$69,646
Resources					
Agriculture	--	--	--	--	--
Coal/Gas/Oil	38	$53,971	$80,184	$106,000	$93,904
Ferrous Mining	--	--	--	--	--
Forestry	--	--	--	--	--
Non-ferrous Mining	--	--	--	--	--
Manufacturing					
Automotive	40	$60,500	$83,250	$119,500	$99,924
Chemical	21	$72,500	$91,000	$110,500	$101,290
Concrete/Clay/Glass/Stone	--	--	--	--	--
Electrical/Electronic	58	$61,000	$83,500	$107,875	$111,802
Food	12	$54,000	$80,684	$119,500	$82,395
Machinery/Metals	19	$50,886	$60,000	$80,368	$76,843
Paper	--	--	--	--	--
Petroleum	24	$49,107	$78,225	$95,698	$84,927
Pharmaceutical	37	$62,000	$86,000	$108,500	$94,313
Plastics	--	--	--	--	--
Textiles/Fabrics	--	--	--	--	--
Wood	--	--	--	--	--
Other Manufacturing	26	$58,000	$74,150	$108,250	$82,198

Compensation by Industry Affiliation

Global

Total Compensation Based on OECD PPP

	N	25th Percentile	Median	75th Percentile	Mean
Construction					
Commercial/Heavy Industrial	129	$57,698	$77,168	$96,486	$83,601
Residential	29	$41,901	$74,534	$99,795	$75,677
Other Construction	36	$62,402	$78,500	$98,300	$80,596
Other Business Activities					
Academia	23	$35,309	$49,000	$95,000	$69,790
Aerospace	32	$70,610	$86,174	$99,034	$86,170
Architecture/Design	50	$56,604	$70,043	$91,208	$75,342
Arts/Entertainment/Broadcasting	--	--	--	--	--
Automation Services	39	$56,104	$65,000	$81,500	$68,989
Business Management	120	$63,044	$80,000	$110,000	$95,206
City Management	--	--	--	--	--
Computers/Software/DP	224	$67,399	$82,750	$105,884	$95,985
Consulting	237	$64,176	$84,000	$108,261	$96,167
Defense	46	$63,034	$74,255	$91,998	$75,536
E-Business	150	$62,500	$79,042	$105,987	$97,715
Economics/Finance	17	$66,200	$75,000	$126,800	$96,411
Education/Training	54	$64,971	$82,500	$114,000	$88,602
Environmental/Waste/Sewage	48	$57,361	$80,000	$97,250	$81,558
Engineering	184	$60,000	$79,230	$96,000	$86,233
Financial Services	101	$63,837	$74,800	$91,500	$79,538
Health/Human/Social Services	39	$42,103	$65,000	$90,000	$71,816
Information Technology	341	$60,905	$77,000	$96,925	$90,667
International Development	24	$69,250	$97,000	$119,250	$105,730
Legal	--	--	--	--	--
Printing/Publishing	--	--	--	--	--
Public Administration/Government	63	$53,000	$66,000	$86,000	$72,793
Real Estate/Insurance	20	$60,000	$71,767	$82,250	$71,902
Recreation	--	--	--	--	--
Supply Chain	37	$65,196	$80,000	$105,000	$88,872
Systems Security	27	$61,499	$70,000	$86,000	$75,838
Telecommunications	199	$58,000	$76,923	$96,000	$79,993
Transportation	49	$64,036	$82,500	$100,750	$89,246
Urban Development	14	$55,439	$87,500	$111,750	$88,836
Utilities	66	$63,827	$83,000	$104,500	$105,115

Compensation by Industry Affiliation

Global
Total Compensation Based on OECD PPP

	N	25th Percentile	Median	75th Percentile	Mean
Other Business Activities (cont.)					
Web Technology	113	$68,000	$80,000	$109,198	$107,311
Other Business Activities	80	$48,706	$68,000	$87,600	$70,872
Resources					
Agriculture	--	--	--	--	--
Coal/Gas/Oil	36	$69,250	$82,500	$109,692	$99,338
Ferrous Mining	--	--	--	--	--
Forestry	--	--	--	--	--
Non-ferrous Mining	--	--	--	--	--
Manufacturing					
Automotive	40	$62,000	$85,000	$116,000	$100,190
Chemical	20	$70,456	$88,424	$110,750	$99,903
Concrete/Clay/Glass/Stone	--	--	--	--	--
Electrical/Electronic	58	$67,250	$85,000	$104,265	$111,512
Food	12	$50,698	$73,600	$119,500	$80,690
Machinery/Metals	19	$52,795	$60,000	$80,000	$76,237
Paper	--	--	--	--	--
Petroleum	22	$57,758	$80,541	$96,500	$89,525
Pharmaceutical	37	$61,696	$85,714	$105,000	$92,815
Plastics	--	--	--	--	--
Textiles/Fabrics	--	--	--	--	--
Wood	--	--	--	--	--
Other Manufacturing	25	$60,000	$76,000	$110,500	$86,541

Compensation by Role in Organization

Average Total Compensation by Role in Organization

Respondents' roles within their organizations were categorized into three broad groups: 1) engineering, 2) management, and 3) other. Thirty-nine (39) specific roles were delineated across these three broad categories. Mean total compensation figures for each of these roles for which there was sufficient data are shown on pages 70 and 71. Roles within an organization that had the highest mean total compensation figures were:

$98,134	Corporate/Administrative
$97,963	Human Resources
$95,644	Earned Value
$95,490	Configuration
$91,373	Consulting

Organizational roles that had the lowest mean total compensation included the following:

$64,539	Web Strategist/Technologist
$68,591	Production
$69,663	Finance
$69,994	Materials
$72,031	Project Accounting/Audit

Compensation by Role in Organization

Global
Total Compensation Based on Exchange Rate

	N	25th Percentile	Median	75th Percentile	Mean
Engineering					
Chemical	--	--	--	--	--
Civil	48	$50,535	$73,150	$99,000	$84,187
Electrical	28	$52,800	$60,535	$98,750	$87,097
Electronics	14	$61,642	$79,684	$89,960	$76,725
Environment	15	$54,000	$70,000	$95,000	$72,780
Industrial	16	$68,250	$77,684	$103,750	$88,435
Mechanical	37	$60,000	$80,000	$101,000	$81,067
Other Engineering	31	$57,554	$65,600	$90,000	$74,278
Management					
Communications	69	$51,750	$76,000	$109,888	$83,610
Configuration	35	$53,000	$79,422	$100,000	$95,490
Contract/Procurement	101	$50,833	$80,000	$108,000	$84,941
Corporate/Administrative	84	$58,205	$80,000	$119,439	$98,134
Cost	99	$55,000	$79,422	$109,776	$83,198
Critical Chain	26	$49,371	$81,184	$108,750	$85,268
Earned Value	53	$58,777	$85,999	$120,000	$95,644
Human Resources	49	$58,454	$80,000	$118,119	$97,963
Information/Computer	182	$60,000	$76,925	$92,000	$80,174
Materials	19	$45,000	$68,999	$91,000	$69,994
Project/Program	703	$55,000	$73,000	$95,000	$81,273
Quality	95	$50,000	$76,000	$96,442	$77,991
Records	23	$39,409	$61,440	$90,000	$79,244
Risk/Safety	58	$59,875	$81,184	$104,253	$86,906
Scope/Technical	101	$44,368	$68,999	$94,897	$78,475
Site/Facility	31	$52,945	$70,000	$90,000	$79,293
Time Management/ Scheduling/Planning	174	$50,000	$74,200	$95,250	$78,237
Other					
Consulting	179	$61,761	$80,368	$107,000	$91,373
Distribution	--	--	--	--	--
Finance	11	$44,115	$70,000	$83,000	$69,663
Financial Services	--	--	--	--	--
Legal	--	--	--	--	--
Marketing/Business Development/Sales	59	$50,600	$75,000	$100,000	$87,263
Production	13	$40,000	$62,500	$98,425	$68,591
Project Accounting/Audit	36	$35,895	$56,876	$82,562	$72,031
Public Relations	--	--	--	--	--
Research/Product Development	39	$52,000	$71,863	$93,777	$81,469
Service & Outsourcing	38	$42,554	$68,734	$92,750	$80,589
Teaching/Training	56	$47,850	$62,500	$98,750	$74,753
Web Strategist/Technologist	11	$36,500	$62,500	$91,000	$64,539
Other	17	$57,000	$80,000	$95,588	$76,979

Compensation by Role in Organization

Global
Total Compensation Based on OECD PPP

	N	25th Percentile	Median	75th Percentile	Mean
Engineering					
Chemical	--	--	--	--	--
Civil	48	$51,715	$70,361	$96,436	$86,796
Electrical	28	$52,800	$61,250	$98,750	$93,531
Electronics	14	$66,598	$72,660	$84,199	$75,773
Environment	15	$52,800	$70,000	$95,000	$71,179
Industrial	16	$68,094	$73,000	$106,378	$88,988
Mechanical	35	$61,000	$76,000	$100,000	$81,627
Other Engineering	31	$60,000	$72,650	$90,000	$78,316
Management					
Communications	69	$52,119	$76,000	$103,750	$83,875
Configuration	35	$55,000	$75,000	$95,000	$99,578
Contract/Procurement	100	$55,980	$76,179	$101,845	$86,465
Corporate/Administrative	84	$62,504	$80,000	$125,000	$102,290
Cost	99	$57,252	$75,000	$98,000	$82,976
Critical Chain	26	$52,096	$85,872	$108,750	$85,874
Earned Value	53	$62,455	$85,999	$120,000	$99,738
Human Resources	49	$62,455	$80,000	$119,829	$101,947
Information/Computer	182	$61,336	$77,250	$93,347	$83,087
Materials	19	$49,200	$68,376	$85,000	$68,646
Project/Program	702	$60,000	$75,214	$96,000	$84,034
Quality	93	$52,895	$74,359	$98,191	$79,786
Records	23	$49,200	$68,999	$91,000	$88,432
Risk/Safety	58	$62,012	$77,743	$105,781	$87,722
Scope/Technical	101	$47,500	$72,650	$92,347	$80,152
Site/Facility	31	$53,000	$74,359	$96,582	$80,574
Time Management/ Scheduling/Planning	174	$50,900	$74,329	$93,147	$78,890
Other					
Consulting	178	$65,995	$82,750	$108,595	$94,635
Distribution	--	--	--	--	--
Finance	11	$47,629	$70,000	$83,000	$71,262
Financial Services	--	--	--	--	--
Legal	--	--	--	--	--
Marketing/Business Development/Sales	59	$55,556	$80,153	$110,000	$94,508
Production	13	$43,581	$62,500	$108,291	$72,613
Project Accounting/Audit	36	$40,377	$63,181	$76,794	$65,163
Public Relations	--	--	--	--	--
Research/Product Development	39	$47,629	$74,359	$93,777	$83,565
Service & Outsourcing	38	$42,977	$72,719	$89,200	$76,055
Teaching/Training	55	$48,000	$71,000	$100,000	$80,204
Web Strategist/Technologist	11	$36,500	$62,500	$110,000	$68,805
Other	17	$57,000	$80,000	$95,588	$77,630

Compensation by Scope of Responsibilities

PMI developed ten scopes of responsibilities, and they are listed in the report as Levels 1 through 10 (see page 11 for definitions). For the most part, the level number was inversely correlated with the level of responsibility, with Level 1 having the highest level of responsibility.

Tables on pages 73 through 77 show mean total compensation by scope of responsibilities. For global and United States data, there were sufficient responses to show analyses by all ten levels plus an eleventh level selected by respondents who felt that none of the other levels adequately described their scopes of responsibilities. For other countries, scopes of responsibilities were condensed into three categories so that there would be sufficient responses for analysis.

For the most part, there was a direct correlation between level of responsibility and mean total compensation. For example, on a global basis, Level 1 had a mean total compensation of $118,876, and values dropped, not quite monotonically, through Level 9. Mean total compensation for Level 10 was influenced upward by a few unusually high values.

A more intuitive relationship between the level of responsibility and mean total compensation is revealed by examining median values. Again, the relationship is not monotonic, yet it is nearly so. The median total compensation for Level 1 was $90,000 and the values drop nearly monotonically to $63,000 for Level 10.

Data for the United States (see page 75) reflect the pattern described above with near monotonic relationships between mean total compensation and level of responsibility. Unusual values that affected global data are also contained within the United States data.

Data for Canada (see page 75) follow the expected pattern with mean total compensation for Levels 1 and 2 exceeding that for Level 3, which in turn, exceeds the value for Levels 4 through 10. Data for other countries and regions of the world follow less intuitive patterns (see pages 76 through 77).

Compensation by Scope of Responsibilities

Comparisons to 1996 [1]

Comparisons to 1996 data are available only for the United States and are shown below. Figures are based on *median* rather than *mean* data to reduce the impact of extreme values on small sample sizes.

Median Total Compensation

	1996	2000	Annual % Increase (Decrease)
Level 1	$97,500	$93,000	(1.2%)
Level 2	$80,500	$95,000	4.5%
Level 3	$70,000	$79,500	3.4%
Level 4	$68,000	$82,500	5.3%
Level 5	$58,000	$77,500	8.4%
Level 6	$63,000	$79,000	6.3%
Level 7	$58,400	$63,000	2.0%
Level 8	$65,000	$60,000	(2.0%)
Level 9	$57,000	$60,500	1.5%
Level 10	$70,000	$74,500	1.6%

Compensation by Scope of Responsibilities

Global

Total Compensation Based on Exchange Rate

	N	25th Percentile	Median	75th Percentile	Mean
Level 1	116	$60,000	$90,000	$124,500	$118,876
Level 2	145	$60,599	$88,300	$110,500	$92,604
Level 3	537	$55,850	$72,500	$91,999	$76,928
Level 4	142	$59,188	$78,187	$99,850	$82,741
Level 5	89	$51,000	$67,500	$83,000	$69,827
Level 6	25	$54,415	$76,083	$99,452	$74,093
Level 7	15	$47,000	$70,000	$80,000	$64,733
Level 8	24	$37,996	$55,650	$75,595	$57,588
Level 9	19	$46,700	$67,520	$89,856	$67,224
Level 10	31	$44,011	$62,000	$86,900	$80,476
Level 11	26	$43,774	$62,500	$80,750	$64,238

Total Compensation Based on OECD PPP

	N	25th Percentile	Median	75th Percentile	Mean
Level 1	116	$66,700	$90,250	$131,000	$122,896
Level 2	145	$69,650	$88,300	$112,750	$95,561
Level 3	536	$60,000	$74,359	$92,030	$79,130
Level 4	141	$63,551	$79,000	$100,000	$84,976
Level 5	89	$57,132	$70,500	$90,000	$75,988
Level 6	25	$56,000	$71,000	$87,500	$73,414
Level 7	15	$47,000	$70,000	$80,000	$65,577
Level 8	24	$40,683	$55,650	$75,595	$59,212
Level 9	19	$46,700	$68,323	$86,500	$66,535
Level 10	28	$55,667	$62,500	$85,925	$84,801
Level 11	26	$48,993	$69,500	$80,750	$67,562

Compensation by Scope of Responsibilities

United States

Total Compensation Based on Exchange Rate

	N	25th Percentile	Median	75th Percentile	Mean
Level 1	54	$78,750	$93,000	$147,000	$129,692
Level 2	91	$82,500	$95,000	$115,000	$99,511
Level 3	336	$66,025	$79,500	$95,000	$82,939
Level 4	85	$68,750	$82,500	$98,350	$86,461
Level 5	53	$62,000	$77,500	$90,500	$78,924
Level 6	15	$59,900	$79,000	$109,000	$78,962
Level 7	11	$45,000	$63,000	$76,510	$62,064
Level 8	13	$53,250	$60,000	$77,500	$64,744
Level 9	10	$52,925	$60,500	$76,050	$64,600
Level 10	19	$59,000	$74,500	$87,000	$96,702
Level 11	12	$62,150	$76,500	$94,375	$78,088

Total Compensation Based on OECD PPP

	N	25th Percentile	Median	75th Percentile	Mean
Level 1	54	$78,750	$93,000	$147,000	$129,692
Level 2	91	$82,500	$95,000	$115,000	$99,511
Level 3	336	$66,025	$79,500	$95,000	$82,939
Level 4	85	$68,750	$82,500	$98,350	$86,461
Level 5	53	$62,000	$77,500	$90,500	$78,924
Level 6	15	$59,900	$79,000	$109,000	$78,962
Level 7	11	$45,000	$63,000	$76,510	$62,064
Level 8	13	$53,250	$60,000	$77,500	$64,744
Level 9	10	$52,925	$60,500	$76,050	$64,600
Level 10	19	$59,000	$74,500	$87,000	$96,702
Level 11	12	$62,150	$76,500	$94,375	$78,088

Canada

Total Compensation Based on Exchange Rate

	N	25th Percentile	Median	75th Percentile	Mean
Levels 1 - 2	35	$47,262	$56,199	$90,000	$78,854
Level 3	75	$44,012	$52,814	$63,648	$59,717
Levels 4 - 10	45	$36,051	$48,278	$57,554	$48,020

Total Compensation Based on OECD PPP

	N	25th Percentile	Median	75th Percentile	Mean
Levels 1 - 2	35	$51,282	$71,795	$90,000	$87,981
Level 3	75	$52,991	$65,231	$76,923	$71,125
Levels 4 - 10	45	$45,513	$57,265	$70,043	$57,666

Compensation by Scope of Responsibilities

Asia

Total Compensation Based on Exchange Rate

	N	25th Percentile	Median	75th Percentile	Mean
Levels 1 - 2	17	$29,000	$96,000	$127,500	$96,163
Level 3	34	$62,375	$93,525	$123,500	$91,951
Levels 4 - 10	29	$63,446	$94,000	$109,730	$104,450

Total Compensation Based on OECD PPP

	N	25th Percentile	Median	75th Percentile	Mean
Levels 1 - 2	17	$98,737	$96,000	$127,500	$98,737
Level 3	34	$62,375	$90,679	$106,692	$84,699
Levels 4 - 10	29	$61,000	$75,000	$105,590	$96,703

Australia/New Zealand

Total Compensation Based on Exchange Rate

	N	25th Percentile	Median	75th Percentile	Mean
Levels 1 - 2	19	$44,115	$50,600	$91,171	$65,131
Level 3	28	$40,038	$50,000	$69,499	$56,422
Levels 4 - 10	21	$38,821	$50,000	$70,584	$70,101

Total Compensation Based on OECD PPP

	N	25th Percentile	Median	75th Percentile	Mean
Levels 1 - 2	19	$50,600	$63,513	$121,622	$81,183
Level 3	28	$50,000	$61,081	$78,959	$66,898
Levels 4 - 10	21	$49,809	$64,885	$90,888	$91,370

Europe

Total Compensation Based on Exchange Rate

	N	25th Percentile	Median	75th Percentile	Mean
Levels 1 - 2	17	$41,250	$61,500	$96,180	$71,828
Level 3	31	$51,356	$64,250	$100,000	$81,255
Levels 4 - 10	24	$43,726	$70,000	$101,242	$74,259

Total Compensation Based on OECD PPP

	N	25th Percentile	Median	75th Percentile	Mean
Levels 1 - 2	17	$37,500	$63,970	$103,050	$71,719
Level 3	31	$51,356	$64,250	$100,000	$81,255
Levels 4 - 10	24	$43,726	$70,000	$101,242	$74,259

Compensation by Scope of Responsibilities

Latin America

Total Compensation Based on Exchange Rate

	N	25th Percentile	Median	75th Percentile	Mean
Levels 1 - 2	15	$70,000	$80,000	$100,000	$133,820
Level 3	20	$26,252	$39,300	$69,168	$49,466
Levels 4 - 10	--	--	--	--	--

Total Compensation Based on OECD PPP

	N	25th Percentile	Median	75th Percentile	Mean
Levels 1 - 2	15	$70,000	$80,000	$100,000	$133,820
Level 3	20	$32,107	$43,200	$71,500	$55,892
Levels 4 - 10	--	--	--	--	--

Middle East

Total Compensation Based on Exchange Rate

	N	25th Percentile	Median	75th Percentile	Mean
Levels 1 - 2	10	$35,775	$70,000	$106,750	$75,714
Level 3	--	--	--	--	--
Levels 4 - 10	11	$37,917	$60,000	$95,843	$67,173

Total Compensation Based on OECD PPP

	N	25th Percentile	Median	75th Percentile	Mean
Levels 1 - 2	10	$35,775	$70,000	$106,750	$75,714
Level 3	--	--	--	--	--
Levels 4 - 10	--	--	--	--	--

Compensation by
Geographic Scope of Projects

Respondents were requested to indicate which of the following categories described the geographic scope of their projects:

> Local,
> State/Province,
> Multi-State/Province,
> Within One Country,
> Multiple Countries, or
> Multiple Continents.

Mean total compensation figures by geographic scope of projects are shown on pages 79 through 82. There was a direct, but not perfect, correlation between mean total compensation on a global basis and geographic scope of projects. For example, the mean total compensation for respondents who were engaged in/managed local projects was $75,818. Mean total compensation increased to $90,948 for respondents who were engaged in/managed projects across multiple continents. Respondents who worked on projects across several countries had the highest mean total compensation ($91,701).

Within the United States, mean total compensation was also highly correlated with geographic scope of projects. Respondents in the United States who were engaged in/managed local projects earned $84,440 in mean total compensation, while those who were engaged in/managed projects across countries and across continents had mean total compensations of $95,431 and $99,885, respectively.

Analyses of mean total compensation by geographic scope of projects was limited in other countries because of small sample sizes. Geographic scope of projects was condensed into two categories: 1) up to and including projects within one country and 2) projects across multiple countries or continents. Results were not always as expected. In Canada, respondents engaged in/managed projects on a limited geographic scale made virtually the same as their counterparts who were engaged in/managed projects across countries or continents. Yet in Europe and Asia, results were more as expected with respondents whose projects involved multiple countries or multiple continents having higher mean total compensation.

Compensation by Geographic Scope of Projects

Comparisons to 1996 [1]

Comparisons to 1996 data are available only for the United States and are shown below. Figures are based on *median* rather than *mean* data to reduce the impact of extreme values on small sample sizes.

Median Total Compensation

	1996	2000	Annual % Increase (Decrease)
Local	$68,000	$77,500	3.5%
State/Province	$73,000	$80,000	2.4%
Multi-State/Province	$72,000	$83,000	3.8%
Within One Country	$73,150	$82,572	3.2%
Multiple Countries	$77,000*	$85,000	2.6%
Multiple Continents	$77,000*	$90,000	4.2%

*In the 1996 study, the delineation "international" was utilized rather than "multiple countries" and "multiple continents."

Compensation by Geographic Scope of Projects

Global

Total Compensation Based on Exchange Rate

	N	25th Percentile	Median	75th Percentile	Mean
Local	426	$51,913	$70,000	$89,250	$75,818
State/Province	260	$50,914	$69,000	$90,000	$78,671
Multi-State/Province	364	$58,023	$76,000	$99,000	$82,653
Within One Country	360	$51,544	$71,048	$94,000	$78,307
Multiple Countries	273	$59,589	$80,000	$100,000	$91,701
Multiple Continents	197	$60,400	$83,000	$109,168	$90,948

Total Compensation Based on OECD PPP

	N	25th Percentile	Median	75th Percentile	Mean
Local	423	$57,000	$72,000	$90,000	$79,152
State/Province	260	$57,255	$72,650	$90,000	$83,107
Multi-State/Province	364	$62,393	$78,000	$99,000	$84,968
Within One Country	356	$57,000	$75,000	$95,000	$81,400
Multiple Countries	272	$62,580	$80,000	$101,500	$94,398
Multiple Continents	197	$62,196	$84,000	$107,198	$91,286

United States

Total Compensation Based on Exchange Rate

	N	25th Percentile	Median	75th Percentile	Mean
Local	264	$61,580	$77,500	$95,750	$84,440
State/Province	147	$65,000	$80,000	$97,600	$88,424
Multi-State/Province	263	$68,000	$83,000	$103,600	$90,317
Within One Country	180	$66,100	$82,572	$97,750	$86,996
Multiple Countries	144	$70,000	$85,000	$104,375	$95,431
Multiple Continents	123	$70,000	$90,000	$112,000	$99,885

Total Compensation Based on OECD PPP

	N	25th Percentile	Median	75th Percentile	Mean
Local	264	$61,580	$77,500	$95,750	$84,440
State/Province	147	$65,000	$80,000	$97,600	$88,424
Multi-State/Province	263	$68,000	$83,000	$103,600	$90,317
Within One Country	180	$66,100	$82,572	$97,750	$86,996
Multiple Countries	144	$70,000	$85,000	$104,375	$95,431
Multiple Continents	123	$70,000	$90,000	$112,000	$99,885

Compensation by Geographic Scope of Projects

Canada

Total Compensation Based on Exchange Rate

	N	25th Percentile	Median	75th Percentile	Mean
Within One Country	131	$44,402	$52,814	$63,500	$61,463
Multiple Countries /Multiple Continents	52	$44,164	$52,907	$63,333	$61,990

Total Compensation Based on OECD PPP

	N	25th Percentile	Median	75th Percentile	Mean
Within One Country	131	$52,400	$65,231	$75,214	$71,968
Multiple Countries /Multiple Continents	52	$50,000	$62,607	$76,495	$67,097

Asia

Total Compensation Based on Exchange Rate

	N	25th Percentile	Median	75th Percentile	Mean
Within One Country	56	$45,000	$88,928	$116,078	$86,405
Multiple Countries /Multiple Continents	34	$80,276	$102,002	$126,250	$153,183

Total Compensation Based on OECD PPP

	N	25th Percentile	Median	75th Percentile	Mean
Within One Country	56	$51,306	$76,179	$105,590	$83,117
Multiple Countries /Multiple Continents	34	$68,360	$85,357	$112,500	$144,531

Australia/New Zealand

Total Compensation Based on Exchange Rate

	N	25th Percentile	Median	75th Percentile	Mean
Within One Country	59	$40,000	$50,000	$67,520	$60,925
Multiple Countries /Multiple Continents	20	$38,674	$56,468	$73,524	$59,885

Total Compensation Based on OECD PPP

	N	25th Percentile	Median	75th Percentile	Mean
Within One Country	59	$50,000	$61,000	$80,534	$75,493
Multiple Countries /Multiple Continents	20	$41,723	$61,060	$95,419	$72,624

Compensation by
Geographic Scope of Projects

Europe

Total Compensation Based on Exchange Rate

	N	25th Percentile	Median	75th Percentile	Mean
Within One Country	42	$39,118	$60,228	$79,466	$67,463
Multiple Countries /Multiple Continents	41	$52,872	$73,294	$104,104	$79,338

Total Compensation Based on OECD PPP

	N	25th Percentile	Median	75th Percentile	Mean
Within One Country	42	$38,059	$59,984	$80,279	$68,067
Multiple Countries /Multiple Continents	41	$52,400	$81,116	$107,113	$82,435

Latin America

Total Compensation Based on Exchange Rate

	N	25th Percentile	Median	75th Percentile	Mean
Within One Country	39	$34,391	$62,517	$81,000	$83,722
Multiple Countries /Multiple Continents	--	--	--	--	--

Total Compensation Based on OECD PPP

	N	25th Percentile	Median	75th Percentile	Mean
Within One Country	39	$37,500	$70,000	$85,000	$87,881
Multiple Countries /Multiple Continents	--	--	--	--	--

Middle East

Total Compensation Based on Exchange Rate

	N	25th Percentile	Median	75th Percentile	Mean
Within One Country	20	$32,897	$52,500	$76,845	$59,100
Multiple Countries /Multiple Continents	--	--	--	--	--

Total Compensation Based on OECD PPP

	N	25th Percentile	Median	75th Percentile	Mean
Within One Country	15	$40,000	$60,000	$77,460	$64,050
Multiple Countries /Multiple Continents	--	--	--	--	--

Compensation by Mean Budget Size of Projects

Page 85 shows mean total compensation by budget size of projects on a global basis. For projects with budgets up to $500 million, there is a direct and strong correlation between budget size of projects and mean total compensation. Respondents working on projects whose budgets were less than $100,000 had a mean total compensation of $68,434. As project budget size increased up to $50 million, respondents' mean total compensation also increased steadily. At this project budget level, respondents' mean total compensation jumped nearly $12,000, and as project budget size increased to the $100 to $500 million range, respondents' mean total compensation jumped over $20,000. At this project budget level, respondents' mean total compensation level declined. It should be noted that sample sizes for projects in the highest budget ranges were small, and results should be interpreted with caution.

Mean total compensation within the United States was also directly correlated with mean budget size of projects. Respondents whose project budgets averaged less than $100,000 had mean total compensation of $74,763, while respondents whose project budgets were over $100 million had mean total compensation of $113,306. Complete results are shown on page 86.

The direct relationship between mean total compensation and project budget size was consistent throughout the world. In Canada, for example, mean total compensation increased from $52,717 for projects with budgets under $500,000 to $77,297 for projects with budgets greater than $25 million (see page 87). Less information was available for other parts of the world.

Compensation by Mean Budget Size of Projects

Comparisons to 1996 [1]

Comparisons to 1996 data are available only for the United States and are shown below. Figures are based on *median* rather than *mean* data to reduce the impact of extreme values on small sample sizes.

Median Total Compensation

	1996	2000	Annual % Increase (Decrease)
<$100,000	$57,500	$70,000	5.4%
$100,000 - $249,999	$62,400	$75,500	5.2%
$250,000 - $499,999	$65,970	$75,000	3.4%
$500,000 - $999,999	$73,224	$79,000	2.0%
$1.0 - $1.99 Million	$68,000	$80,615	4.6%
$2.0 - $2.99 Million	$72,000	$86,000	4.9%
$3.0 - $3.99 Million	$73,201	$86,000	4.4%
$4.0 - $4.99 Million	$67,500	$98,400	11.4%
$5.0 - $9.99 Million	$70,000	$83,072	4.7%
$10.0 - $24.99 Million	$80,500	$89,549	2.8%
$25.0 - $49.99 Million	$74,150	$85,000	3.7%
$50.0 - $99.99 Million	$83,000	$84,500	0.5%
$100.0 - $499.99 Million	$84,000	$97,500	4.0%

Compensation by Mean Budget Size of Projects

Global

Total Compensation Based on Exchange Rate

	N	25th Percentile	Median	75th Percentile	Mean
<$100,000	113	$46,506	$62,000	$88,500	$68,434
$100,000 - $249,000	123	$48,000	$70,000	$82,000	$71,257
$250,000 - $499,999	117	$41,709	$63,527	$85,500	$72,174
$500,000 - $999,999	116	$60,374	$75,580	$90,750	$78,823
$1.0 Million - $1.99 Million	119	$60,262	$75,000	$94,000	$77,218
$2.0 Million - $2.99 Million	86	$60,805	$78,600	$95,475	$83,009
$3.0 Million - $3.99 Million	55	$57,300	$76,000	$103,905	$80,201
$4.0 Million - $4.99 Million	35	$57,554	$88,000	$114,000	$84,167
$5.0 Million - $9.99 Million	107	$60,319	$78,000	$92,040	$86,656
$10.0 Million - $24.99 Million	95	$58,200	$82,000	$106,000	$89,597
$25.0 Million - $49.99 Million	52	$57,050	$80,000	$120,000	$87,955
$50.0 Million - $99.99 Million	52	$62,670	$81,500	$105,750	$99,601
$100.0 Million - $499.99 Million	67	$69,000	$90,000	$115,000	$120,532
$500.0 Million - $999.99 Million	17	$70,880	$80,000	$110,000	$92,055
$1.0 Billion - $9.99 Billion	11	$81,313	$88,000	$100,000	$90,719
≥$10.0 Billion	--	--	--	--	--

Total Compensation Based on OECD PPP

	N	25th Percentile	Median	75th Percentile	Mean
<$100,000	113	$49,787	$65,000	$89,372	$71,292
$100,000 - $249,000	123	$51,000	$70,000	$82,000	$72,734
$250,000 - $499,999	117	$49,409	$67,500	$87,750	$76,004
$500,000 - $999,999	116	$63,625	$78,000	$95,718	$81,339
$1.0 Million - $1.99 Million	119	$66,400	$75,214	$95,000	$80,162
$2.0 Million - $2.99 Million	86	$65,358	$80,577	$101,000	$88,170
$3.0 Million - $3.99 Million	54	$63,256	$79,500	$104,625	$86,316
$4.0 Million - $4.99 Million	35	$61,500	$83,000	$111,000	$85,274
$5.0 Million - $9.99 Million	107	$61,000	$80,000	$100,000	$89,660
$10.0 Million - $24.99 Million	94	$59,747	$82,250	$106,250	$90,872
$25.0 Million - $49.99 Million	52	$62,125	$80,000	$118,500	$89,179
$50.0 Million - $99.99 Million	52	$69,250	$81,500	$105,750	$100,094
$100.0 Million - $499.99 Million	66	$68,816	$86,750	$115,000	$121,454
$500.0 Million - $999.99 Million	16	$74,615	$89,928	$106,526	$95,152
$1.0 Billion - $9.99 Billion	11	$76,000	$88,000	$100,000	$88,183
≥$10.0 Billion	--	--	--	--	--

Compensation by Mean Budget Size of Projects

United States

Total Compensation Based on Exchange Rate

	N	25th Percentile	Median	75th Percentile	Mean
<$100,000	72	$56,014	$70,000	$90,750	$74,763
$100,000 - $249,000	72	$63,000	$75,500	$87,500	$75,786
$250,000 - $499,999	67	$63,000	$75,000	$92,000	$79,792
$500,000 - $999,999	75	$67,468	$79,000	$97,600	$83,934
$1.0 Million - $1.99 Million	82	$67,150	$80,615	$97,175	$83,572
$2.0 Million - $2.99 Million	54	$70,000	$86,000	$97,750	$88,210
$3.0 Million - $3.99 Million	34	$70,000	$86,000	$112,500	$93,233
$4.0 Million - $4.99 Million	23	$80,000	$98,400	$118,000	$96,322
$5.0 Million - $9.99 Million	62	$65,000	$83,072	$101,000	$98,013
$10.0 Million - $24.99 Million	54	$63,750	$89,549	$110,325	$100,226
$25.0 Million - $49.99 Million	24	$68,785	$85,000	$120,375	$99,528
$50.0 Million - $99.99 Million	24	$70,500	$84,500	$123,750	$105,442
$100.0 Million - $499.99 Million	34	$77,250	$97,500	$120,000	$113,306
$500.0 Million - $999.99 Million	--	--	--	--	--
$1.0 Billion - $9.99 Billion	--	--	--	--	--
≥$10.0 Billion	--	--	--	--	--

Total Compensation Based on OECD PPP

	N	25th Percentile	Median	75th Percentile	Mean
<$100,000	72	$56,014	$70,000	$90,750	$74,763
$100,000 - $249,000	72	$63,000	$75,500	$87,500	$75,786
$250,000 - $499,999	67	$63,000	$75,000	$92,000	$79,792
$500,000 - $999,999	75	$67,468	$79,000	$97,600	$83,934
$1.0 Million - $1.99 Million	82	$67,150	$80,615	$97,175	$83,572
$2.0 Million - $2.99 Million	54	$70,000	$86,000	$97,750	$88,210
$3.0 Million - $3.99 Million	34	$70,000	$86,000	$112,500	$93,233
$4.0 Million - $4.99 Million	23	$80,000	$98,400	$118,000	$96,322
$5.0 Million - $9.99 Million	62	$65,000	$83,072	$101,000	$98,013
$10.0 Million - $24.99 Million	54	$63,750	$89,549	$110,325	$100,226
$25.0 Million - $49.99 Million	24	$68,785	$85,000	$120,375	$99,528
$50.0 Million - $99.99 Million	24	$70,500	$84,500	$123,750	$105,442
$100.0 Million - $499.99 Million	34	$77,250	$97,500	$120,000	$113,306
$500.0 Million - $999.99 Million	--	--	--	--	--
$1.0 Billion - $9.99 Billion	--	--	--	--	--
≥$10.0 Billion	--	--	--	--	--

Compensation by Mean
Budget Size of Projects

Canada

Total Compensation Based on Exchange Rate

	N	25th Percentile	Median	75th Percentile	Mean
<$500,000	62	$35,207	$46,998	$57,554	$52,717
$500,000 - $1.99 Million	33	$48,699	$54,169	$63,824	$63,523
$2.0 Million - $24.99 Million	31	$46,043	$59,505	$76,000	$67,703
≥$25.0 Million	17	$44,011	$56,199	$85,653	$77,297

Total Compensation Based on OECD PPP

	N	25th Percentile	Median	75th Percentile	Mean
<$500,000	62	$43,055	$51,841	$68,782	$57,237
$500,000 - $1.99 Million	33	$57,692	$67,949	$75,607	$71,820
$2.0 Million - $24.99 Million	31	$58,119	$70,086	$79,487	$77,125
≥$25.0 Million	17	$55,556	$70,940	$108,120	$90,645

Asia

Total Compensation Based on Exchange Rate

	N	25th Percentile	Median	75th Percentile	Mean
<$500,000	--	--	--	--	--
$500,000 - $1.99 Million	--	--	--	--	--
$2.0 Million - $24.99 Million	22	$57,750	$103,955	$118,428	$89,343
≥$25.0 Million	40	$76,855	$95,500	$125,250	$134,395

Total Compensation Based on OECD PPP

	N	25th Percentile	Median	75th Percentile	Mean
<$500,000	--	--	--	--	--
$500,000 - $1.99 Million	--	--	--	--	--
$2.0 Million - $24.99 Million	22	$52,031	$81,957	$111,400	$84,042
≥$25.0 Million	40	$65,830	$82,500	$105,897	$125,676

Compensation by Mean
Budget Size of Projects

Australia/New Zealand

Total Compensation Based on Exchange Rate

	N	25th Percentile	Median	75th Percentile	Mean
<$500,000	25	$36,762	$44,406	$56,469	$62,284
$500,000 - $1.99 Million	11	$42,437	$61,976	$79,363	$59,444
$2.0 Million - $24.99 Million	22	$46,279	$61,349	$89,407	$66,903
≥$25.0 Million	--	--	--	--	--

Total Compensation Based on OECD PPP

	N	25th Percentile	Median	75th Percentile	Mean
<$500,000	25	$42,905	$51,185	$65,756	$75,534
$500,000 - $1.99 Million	11	$63,000	$87,029	$113,513	$84,070
$2.0 Million - $24.99 Million	22	$54,578	$68,500	$102,099	$78,413
≥$25.0 Million	--	--	--	--	--

Europe

Total Compensation Based on Exchange Rate

	N	25th Percentile	Median	75th Percentile	Mean
<$500,000	21	$29,640	$48,928	$79,644	$56,591
$500,000 - $1.99 Million	12	$57,000	$70,000	$99,390	$74,276
$2.0 Million - $24.99 Million	26	$52,634	$61,035	$87,210	$69,579
≥$25.0 Million	12	$69,250	$82,254	$156,893	$109,263

Total Compensation Based on OECD PPP

	N	25th Percentile	Median	75th Percentile	Mean
<$500,000	21	$31,034	$47,704	$93,058	$61,081
$500,000 - $1.99 Million	12	$57,000	$70,000	$100,000	$74,492
$2.0 Million - $24.99 Million	26	$52,439	$66,985	$88,102	$70,900
≥$25.0 Million	12	$69,250	$81,657	$154,997	$109,924

Compensation by Mean Budget Size of Projects

Latin America

Total Compensation Based on Exchange Rate

	N	25th Percentile	Median	75th Percentile	Mean
<$500,000	--	--	--	--	--
$500,000 - $1.99 Million	--	--	--	--	--
$2.0 Million - $24.99 Million	21	$35,945	$50,886	$77,150	$59,858
≥$25.0 Million	10	$33,000	$78,000	$96,000	$68,000

Total Compensation Based on OECD PPP

	N	25th Percentile	Median	75th Percentile	Mean
<$500,000	--	--	--	--	--
$500,000 - $1.99 Million	--	--	--	--	--
$2.0 Million - $24.99 Million	21	$41,300	$56,493	$80,000	$66,976
≥$25.0 Million	10	$33,000	$78,000	$96,000	$68,000

Middle East

Total Compensation Based on Exchange Rate

	N	25th Percentile	Median	75th Percentile	Mean
<$500,000	--	--	--	--	--
$500,000 - $1.99 Million	--	--	--	--	--
$2.0 Million - $24.99 Million	11	$40,000	$75,000	$96,444	$72,128
≥$25.0 Million	13	$40,198	$60,000	$99,000	$73,509

Total Compensation Based on OECD PPP

	N	25th Percentile	Median	75th Percentile	Mean
<$500,000	--	--	--	--	--
$500,000 - $1.99 Million	--	--	--	--	--
$2.0 Million - $24.99 Million	--	--	--	--	--
≥$25.0 Million	11	$50,000	$65,000	$100,000	$80,174

Compensation by Number of Projects Engaged In/Managed

On a global basis, there was a correlation between mean total compensation and the number of projects in which respondents were engaged in or managed (see page 91). Yet the difference in mean total compensation across numbers of projects engaged in/managed was not substantial. For example, respondents who were engaged in/managed only 1 project had a mean total compensation of $80,119, while respondents who were engaged in/managed over 10 projects had a mean total compensation of $86,437.

Within the United States, the relationship between number of projects engaged in/managed and mean total compensation was not linear nor predictable. Respondents who were engaged in/managed only 1 project had a mean total compensation of $84,654, while those who were engaged in/managed over 10 projects had a mean total compensation of $84,226. Surprisingly, respondents who were engaged in/managed 2 projects had a mean total compensation of $92,893.

The relationship between mean total compensation and number of projects engaged in/managed varied based on the region of the world examined. In Asia, higher mean total compensation was associated with managing or working with more projects. In Canada and Europe, this was not the case.

Sample sizes were comfortably large for each level of analysis within the United States, so that unexpected results for this question cannot be blamed on small sample sizes. The unusual and unexpected relationship between mean total compensation and number of projects engaged in/managed may have resulted from other factors not captured in this study.

Compensation by Number of Projects Engaged In/Managed

Global

Total Compensation Based on Exchange Rate

	N	25th Percentile	Median	75th Percentile	Mean
1 Project	161	$57,554	$75,000	$95,921	$80,119
2 Projects	194	$55,392	$71,000	$96,486	$81,977
3 Projects	221	$56,000	$75,000	$94,000	$86,928
4 Projects	122	$52,255	$70,000	$90,999	$74,230
5 Projects	106	$53,625	$80,184	$95,361	$78,656
6 - 10 Projects	169	$59,545	$78,000	$101,500	$86,721
11+ Projects	145	$51,619	$75,159	$100,000	$86,437

Total Compensation Based on OECD PPP

	N	25th Percentile	Median	75th Percentile	Mean
1 Project	159	$63,970	$75,000	$95,000	$81,998
2 Projects	193	$60,277	$75,000	$97,800	$85,346
3 Projects	220	$60,000	$76,679	$96,233	$89,675
4 Projects	122	$55,442	$70,896	$91,000	$77,311
5 Projects	106	$57,197	$80,000	$95,000	$80,320
6 - 10 Projects	169	$61,500	$78,000	$104,300	$88,569
11+ Projects	144	$57,698	$78,787	$99,500	$87,711

United States

Total Compensation Based on Exchange Rate

	N	25th Percentile	Median	75th Percentile	Mean
1 Project	90	$65,300	$79,000	$96,500	$84,654
2 Projects	109	$69,000	$81,400	$100,000	$92,893
3 Projects	129	$65,000	$78,900	$93,600	$86,936
4 Projects	72	$66,125	$80,750	$95,000	$85,029
5 Projects	61	$69,009	$85,000	$95,750	$84,626
6 - 10 Projects	117	$69,356	$84,000	$110,750	$94,179
11+ Projects	90	$64,500	$82,750	$101,125	$84,226

Total Compensation Based on OECD PPP

	N	25th Percentile	Median	75th Percentile	Mean
1 Project	90	$65,300	$79,000	$96,500	$84,654
2 Projects	109	$69,000	$81,400	$100,000	$92,893
3 Projects	129	$65,000	$78,900	$93,600	$86,936
4 Projects	72	$66,125	$80,750	$95,000	$85,029
5 Projects	61	$69,009	$85,000	$95,750	$84,626
6 - 10 Projects	117	$69,356	$84,000	$110,750	$94,179
11+ Projects	90	$64,500	$82,750	$101,125	$84,226

Compensation by Number of Projects Engaged In/Managed

Canada

Total Compensation Based on Exchange Rate

	N	25th Percentile	Median	75th Percentile	Mean
1 - 2 Projects	53	$45,332	$54,000	$63,021	$59,912
3 - 7 Projects	64	$43,523	$52,907	$72,149	$64,716
8+ Projects	38	$37,173	$49,598	$61,704	$62,249

Total Compensation Based on OECD PPP

	N	25th Percentile	Median	75th Percentile	Mean
1 - 2 Projects	53	$53,495	$67,949	$76,461	$71,628
3 - 7 Projects	64	$51,711	$64,957	$79,871	$75,241
8+ Projects	38	$44,123	$52,700	$72,387	$62,385

Asia

Total Compensation Based on Exchange Rate

	N	25th Percentile	Median	75th Percentile	Mean
1 - 2 Projects	30	$47,625	$94,025	$109,484	$86,435
3 - 7 Projects	40	$63,125	$84,197	$119,059	$135,238
8+ Projects	--	--	--	--	--

Total Compensation Based on OECD PPP

	N	25th Percentile	Median	75th Percentile	Mean
1 - 2 Projects	30	$54,125	$68,668	$105,750	$93,221
3 - 7 Projects	40	$55,096	$76,056	$105,590	$127,438
8+ Projects	--	--	--	--	--

Australia/New Zealand

Total Compensation Based on Exchange Rate

	N	25th Percentile	Median	75th Percentile	Mean
1 - 2 Projects	25	$42,317	$60,937	$68,703	$57,192
3 - 7 Projects	31	$39,409	$50,000	$74,113	$56,430
8+ Projects	13	$39,854	$42,516	$84,115	$81,748

Total Compensation Based on OECD PPP

	N	25th Percentile	Median	75th Percentile	Mean
1 - 2 Projects	25	$51,717	$67,176	$83,781	$70,377
3 - 7 Projects	31	$45,802	$57,432	$96,183	$70,371
8+ Projects	13	$49,809	$60,811	$102,977	$107,042

Compensation by Number of Projects Engaged In/Managed

Europe

Total Compensation Based on Exchange Rate

	N	25th Percentile	Median	75th Percentile	Mean
1 - 2 Projects	29	$56,137	$70,000	$111,604	$88,350
3 - 7 Projects	32	$35,806	$54,500	$88,011	$62,119
8+ Projects	--	--	--	--	--

Total Compensation Based on OECD PPP

	N	25th Percentile	Median	75th Percentile	Mean
1 - 2 Projects	29	$55,384	$70,000	$110,828	$88,439
3 - 7 Projects	32	$38,988	$54,500	$87,011	$63,304
8+ Projects	--	--	--	--	--

Latin America

Total Compensation Based on Exchange Rate

	N	25th Percentile	Median	75th Percentile	Mean
1 - 2 Projects	--	--	--	--	--
3 - 7 Projects	31	$30,000	$62,517	$85,000	$64,360
8+ Projects	--	--	--	--	--

Total Compensation Based on OECD PPP

	N	25th Percentile	Median	75th Percentile	Mean
1 - 2 Projects	--	--	--	--	--
3 - 7 Projects	31	$34,000	$62,517	$87,800	$68,506
8+ Projects	--	--	--	--	--

Middle East

Total Compensation Based on Exchange Rate

	N	25th Percentile	Median	75th Percentile	Mean
1 - 2 Projects	10	$36,242	$65,000	$108,132	$75,345
3 - 7 Projects	10	$35,934	$55,000	$96,833	$62,588
8+ Projects	--	--	--	--	--

Total Compensation Based on OECD PPP

	N	25th Percentile	Median	75th Percentile	Mean
1 - 2 Projects	--	--	--	--	--
3 - 7 Projects	--	--	--	--	--
8+ Projects	--	--	--	--	--

Compensation by Number of Employees Supervised

On a global basis, there was a correlation between mean total compensation and number of employees supervised. As number of employees supervised increased, mean total compensation rose steadily (from $70,839 to $87,144) until a respondent supervised over 50 employees. At this point, mean total compensation increased dramatically to $123,829.

Within the United States, this same relationship existed with mean total compensation rising from $78,199 (with one or two subordinates) to $92,347 (with 26 to 50 subordinates). Respondents who supervised over 50 employees had a mean total compensation of $115,829.

The direct and strong correlation between mean total compensation and number of employees supervised held for Canada, Asia, and Europe, but not for Australia/New Zealand and Latin America.

Compensation by Number of Employees Supervised

Global

Total Compensation Based on Exchange Rate

	N	25th Percentile	Median	75th Percentile	Mean
1 - 2 People Supervised	67	$50,600	$72,000	$86,000	$70,839
3 - 4 People Supervised	93	$53,915	$75,000	$95,000	$80,897
5 - 6 People Supervised	104	$57,665	$75,000	$94,750	$82,581
7 - 8 People Supervised	85	$55,084	$77,000	$98,850	$80,124
9 - 10 People Supervised	90	$49,999	$70,500	$86,500	$81,782
11 - 15 People Supervised	124	$60,000	$79,000	$99,225	$78,986
16 - 20 People Supervised	87	$51,000	$75,000	$104,000	$80,191
21 - 25 People Supervised	61	$59,250	$75,000	$100,500	$82,941
26 - 50 People Supervised	93	$59,752	$82,500	$101,500	$87,144
51+ People Supervised	72	$75,717	$95,722	$127,750	$123,829

Total Compensation Based on OECD PPP

	N	25th Percentile	Median	75th Percentile	Mean
1 - 2 People Supervised	66	$53,858	$72,250	$86,500	$72,712
3 - 4 People Supervised	93	$58,540	$75,000	$95,000	$83,790
5 - 6 People Supervised	104	$62,794	$75,000	$93,000	$84,862
7 - 8 People Supervised	85	$61,769	$78,000	$100,500	$84,302
9 - 10 People Supervised	90	$56,078	$71,500	$86,257	$83,789
11 - 15 People Supervised	123	$65,000	$80,000	$103,000	$83,284
16 - 20 People Supervised	86	$60,621	$78,500	$105,500	$84,136
21 - 25 People Supervised	61	$59,250	$80,000	$100,500	$84,264
26 - 50 People Supervised	93	$60,750	$83,144	$107,692	$89,359
51+ People Supervised	72	$75,135	$95,722	$123,000	$124,002

Compensation by Number of Employees Supervised

United States

Total Compensation Based on Exchange Rate

	N	25th Percentile	Median	75th Percentile	Mean
1 - 2 People Supervised	44	$63,900	$77,500	$90,750	$78,199
3 - 4 People Supervised	57	$68,250	$84,000	$97,500	$92,855
5 - 6 People Supervised	59	$66,200	$78,000	$98,000	$87,200
7 - 8 People Supervised	49	$69,500	$90,000	$114,500	$93,215
9 - 10 People Supervised	47	$65,500	$77,000	$90,000	$96,296
11 - 15 People Supervised	72	$72,875	$87,500	$109,888	$91,753
16 - 20 People Supervised	40	$74,850	$86,500	$111,500	$91,763
21 - 25 People Supervised	40	$68,500	$84,300	$104,500	$92,731
26 - 50 People Supervised	50	$67,025	$89,000	$112,225	$92,347
51+ People Supervised	39	$85,000	$100,000	$127,000	$115,829

Total Compensation Based on OECD PPP

	N	25th Percentile	Median	75th Percentile	Mean
1 - 2 People Supervised	44	$63,900	$77,500	$90,750	$78,199
3 - 4 People Supervised	57	$68,250	$84,000	$97,500	$92,855
5 - 6 People Supervised	59	$66,200	$78,000	$98,000	$87,200
7 - 8 People Supervised	49	$69,500	$90,000	$114,500	$93,215
9 - 10 People Supervised	47	$65,500	$77,000	$90,000	$96,296
11 - 15 People Supervised	72	$72,875	$87,500	$109,888	$91,753
16 - 20 People Supervised	40	$74,850	$86,500	$111,500	$91,763
21 - 25 People Supervised	40	$68,500	$84,300	$104,500	$92,731
26 - 50 People Supervised	50	$67,025	$89,000	$112,225	$92,347
51+ People Supervised	39	$85,000	$100,000	$127,000	$115,829

Compensation by Number of Employees Supervised

Canada

Total Compensation Based on Exchange Rate

	N	25th Percentile	Median	75th Percentile	Mean
1 - 5 People Supervised	33	$40,440	$50,783	$73,250	$57,134
6 - 24 People Supervised	73	$49,090	$53,000	$62,682	$63,864
25+ People Supervised	17	$57,215	$71,095	$85,314	$86,177

Total Compensation Based on OECD PPP

	N	25th Percentile	Median	75th Percentile	Mean
1 - 5 People Supervised	33	$50,042	$64,103	$75,461	$68,383
6 - 24 People Supervised	73	$53,500	$65,812	$75,607	$73,951
25+ People Supervised	17	$72,991	$82,000	$107,692	$101,131

Asia

Total Compensation Based on Exchange Rate

	N	25th Percentile	Median	75th Percentile	Mean
1 - 5 People Supervised	13	$77,820	$85,000	$105,002	$94,573
6 - 24 People Supervised	33	$31,860	$66,302	$104,005	$68,673
25+ People Supervised	21	$85,736	$113,460	$156,008	$171,702

Total Compensation Based on OECD PPP

	N	25th Percentile	Median	75th Percentile	Mean
1 - 5 People Supervised	13	$68,323	$68,323	$80,000	$90,857
6 - 24 People Supervised	33	$43,239	$43,239	$68,323	$88,706
25+ People Supervised	21	$69,823	$69,823	$100,000	$127,500

Australia/New Zealand

Total Compensation Based on Exchange Rate

	N	25th Percentile	Median	75th Percentile	Mean
1 - 5 People Supervised	15	$38,233	$41,174	$51,964	$69,121
6 - 24 People Supervised	33	$43,933	$50,000	$68,703	$57,751
25+ People Supervised	--	--	--	--	--

Total Compensation Based on OECD PPP

	N	25th Percentile	Median	75th Percentile	Mean
1 - 5 People Supervised	15	$40,541	$50,600	$79,084	$90,165
6 - 24 People Supervised	33	$53,644	$66,216	$87,407	$70,672
25+ People Supervised	--	--	--	--	--

Compensation by Number
of Employees Supervised

Europe

Total Compensation Based on Exchange Rate

	N	25th Percentile	Median	75th Percentile	Mean
1 - 5 People Supervised	13	$38,821	$47,200	$85,932	$61,937
6 - 24 People Supervised	31	$48,928	$61,500	$86,000	$69,970
25+ People Supervised	16	$50,736	$63,182	$95,341	$84,831

Total Compensation Based on OECD PPP

	N	25th Percentile	Median	75th Percentile	Mean
1 - 5 People Supervised	13	$37,382	$47,704	$85,397	$63,413
6 - 24 People Supervised	31	$48,946	$63,970	$86,000	$70,554
25+ People Supervised	16	$45,369	$63,000	$98,077	$84,252

Latin America

Total Compensation Based on Exchange Rate

	N	25th Percentile	Median	75th Percentile	Mean
1 - 5 People Supervised	--	--	--	--	--
6 - 24 People Supervised	22	$33,000	$68,336	$96,000	$69,958
25+ People Supervised	21	$39,050	$62,517	$80,500	$64,947

Total Compensation Based on OECD PPP

	N	25th Percentile	Median	75th Percentile	Mean
1 - 5 People Supervised	--	--	--	--	--
6 - 24 People Supervised	22	$33,285	$71,000	$99,500	$74,639
25+ People Supervised	21	$41,300	$70,000	$80,500	$67,162

Compensation by Number of People in Project Management at Location

On a global basis, there was a correlation between mean total compensation and number of people in project management at respondents' worksites. However, there were anomalies in the relationship. Respondents who had only 1 or 2 other people in project management at their location had a higher mean total compensation than their counterparts, who had 3 or 4 people or 16 to 30 people in project management at their sites.

Within the United States, the relationship between number of people in project management at members' worksites and mean total compensation was nearly random. Respondents within the United States who had only 1 or 2 other people in project management at their worksites had the highest mean total compensation. With the exception of a few anomalies, there appeared to be a uniform relationship between mean total compensation and number of people in project management at respondents' worksites.

After examining data from other areas of the world, Asia was the only area that exhibited a direct and strong correlation between mean total compensation and number of people in project management at respondents' worksites.

Compensation by Number of People in Project Management at Location

Global

Total Compensation Based on Exchange Rate

	N	25th Percentile	Median	75th Percentile	Mean
1 - 2 People	101	$49,314	$65,600	$91,250	$79,549
3 - 4 People	127	$52,000	$69,000	$91,000	$70,970
5 - 10 People	302	$57,466	$77,000	$98,000	$83,173
11 - 15 People	111	$60,000	$80,000	$97,500	$85,413
16 - 20 People	93	$51,500	$75,000	$94,797	$79,370
21 - 30 People	108	$50,108	$70,500	$97,237	$78,212
31+ People	254	$59,125	$79,100	$96,558	$90,384

Total Compensation Based on OECD PPP

	N	25th Percentile	Median	75th Percentile	Mean
1 - 2 People	101	$55,000	$70,000	$94,936	$83,644
3 - 4 People	127	$54,000	$70,500	$91,000	$73,229
5 - 10 People	300	$61,499	$79,000	$98,300	$86,816
11 - 15 People	109	$65,056	$81,196	$100,500	$88,404
16 - 20 People	93	$55,632	$75,000	$100,000	$82,110
21 - 30 People	107	$56,600	$73,333	$96,000	$79,333
31+ People	254	$61,750	$79,142	$96,925	$91,662

United States

Total Compensation Based on Exchange Rate

	N	25th Percentile	Median	75th Percentile	Mean
1 - 2 People	59	$60,000	$80,000	$100,000	$93,518
3 - 4 People	81	$64,500	$76,000	$95,625	$79,180
5 - 10 People	195	$66,400	$82,500	$100,000	$88,035
11 - 15 People	72	$70,000	$83,000	$100,750	$93,511
16 - 20 People	49	$65,460	$79,000	$92,100	$86,313
21 - 30 People	54	$65,000	$84,500	$97,625	$83,549
31+ People	146	$69,750	$81,750	$99,250	$89,547

Total Compensation Based on OECD PPP

	N	25th Percentile	Median	75th Percentile	Mean
1 - 2 People	59	$60,000	$80,000	$100,000	$93,518
3 - 4 People	81	$64,500	$76,000	$95,625	$79,180
5 - 10 People	195	$66,400	$82,500	$100,000	$88,035
11 - 15 People	72	$70,000	$83,000	$100,750	$93,511
16 - 20 People	49	$65,460	$79,000	$92,100	$86,313
21 - 30 People	54	$65,000	$84,500	$97,625	$83,549
31+ People	146	$69,750	$81,750	$99,250	$89,547

Compensation by Number of People in Project Management at Location

Canada

Total Compensation Based on Exchange Rate

	N	25th Percentile	Median	75th Percentile	Mean
1 - 10 People	81	$42,761	$52,137	$67,371	$60,979
11 - 50 People	61	$40,440	$52,400	$60,266	$56,910
51+ People	13	$47,500	$57,554	$74,000	$62,580

Total Compensation Based on OECD PPP

	N	25th Percentile	Median	75th Percentile	Mean
1 - 10 People	81	$51,901	$62,393	$75,179	$71,202
11 - 50 People	61	$47,436	$64,103	$76,068	$67,971
51+ People	13	$52,778	$70,940	$75,325	$71,142

Asia

Total Compensation Based on Exchange Rate

	N	25th Percentile	Median	75th Percentile	Mean
1 - 10 People	27	$35,720	$80,000	$110,000	$71,202
11 - 50 People	25	$64,039	$10,000	$124,000	$93,819
51+ People	21	$70,961	$95,000	$148,367	$170,864

Total Compensation Based on OECD PPP

	N	25th Percentile	Median	75th Percentile	Mean
1 - 10 People	27	$49,742	$80,000	$105,590	$92,808
11 - 50 People	25	$60,522	$75,000	$112,445	$85,401
51+ People	21	$53,105	$94,000	$118,000	$162,285

Australia/New Zealand

Total Compensation Based on Exchange Rate

	N	25th Percentile	Median	75th Percentile	Mean
1 - 10 People	30	$42,121	$50,300	$68,499	$65,963
11 - 50 People	24	$39,781	$45,351	$67,390	$55,339
51+ People	10	$34,381	$62,488	$87,789	$65,012

Total Compensation Based on OECD PPP

	N	25th Percentile	Median	75th Percentile	Mean
1 - 10 People	30	$50,000	$60,534	$80,698	$80,344
11 - 50 People	24	$46,756	$61,581	$90,532	$70,211
51+ People	10	$45,669	$79,809	$113,930	$82,522

Compensation by Number of People in Project Management at Location

Europe

Total Compensation Based on Exchange Rate

	N	25th Percentile	Median	75th Percentile	Mean
1 - 10 People	23	$39,416	$60,319	$80,000	$70,131
11 - 50 People	33	$46,346	$70,000	$96,180	$74,481
51+ People	13	$46,536	$60,555	$102,841	$73,950

Total Compensation Based on OECD PPP

	N	25th Percentile	Median	75th Percentile	Mean
1 - 10 People	23	$44,615	$61,500	$100,000	$74,995
11 - 50 People	33	$45,973	$70,000	$100,000	$75,956
51+ People	13	$45,064	$60,555	$102,174	$73,285

Latin America

Total Compensation Based on Exchange Rate

	N	25th Percentile	Median	75th Percentile	Mean
1 - 10 People	16	$20,574	$50,008	$92,000	$58,427
11 - 50 People	16	$31,375	$54,443	$84,600	$67,815
51+ People	12	$43,950	$76,000	$84,000	$131,466

Total Compensation Based on OECD PPP

	N	25th Percentile	Median	75th Percentile	Mean
1 - 10 People	16	$28,035	$56,505	$92,000	$60,603
11 - 50 People	16	$37,125	$64,913	$69,650	$75,775
51+ People	12	$43,950	$76,000	$84,000	$131,466

Middle East

Total Compensation Based on Exchange Rate

	N	25th Percentile	Median	75th Percentile	Mean
1 - 10 People	11	$40,000	$66,000	$98,000	$68,175
11 - 50 People	11	$24,999	$55,000	$133,000	$71,870
51+ People	--	--	--	--	--

Total Compensation Based on OECD PPP

	N	25th Percentile	Median	75th Percentile	Mean
1 - 10 People	--	--	--	--	--
11 - 50 People	--	--	--	--	--
51+ People	--	--	--	--	--

Compensation by Number of People in Project Management in Organization

While respondents who had the largest number of people in project management in their organizations had the highest average total compensation, there was not a strong correlation on a global basis between mean total compensation and number of people in project management in respondents' organizations. The lack of relationship between mean total compensation and number of people in project management in respondents' organizations held true within the United States. However in Europe, Asia, and Australia/New Zealand, there was a direct correlation between mean total compensation and number of people in project management in respondents' organizations.

Compensation by Number of People in Project Management in Organization

Global

Total Compensation Based on Exchange Rate

	N	25th Percentile	Median	75th Percentile	Mean
1 - 10 People	190	$49,150	$71,000	$96,000	$80,422
11 - 25 People	129	$58,550	$78,375	$90,999	$77,754
26 - 50 People	147	$52,800	$72,500	$98,000	$83,850
51 - 100 People	126	$53,625	$76,000	$95,000	$77,281
101 - 300 People	114	$60,750	$80,532	$100,000	$75,433
301+ People	196	$60,000	$77,250	$102,906	$88,256

Total Compensation Based on OECD PPP

	N	25th Percentile	Median	75th Percentile	Mean
1 - 10 People	189	$53,717	$72,000	$96,125	$83,776
11 - 25 People	129	$60,000	$78,375	$92,000	$80,247
26 - 50 People	146	$61,878	$72,500	$98,000	$85,720
51 - 100 People	125	$59,706	$76,000	$94,500	$79,030
101 - 300 People	114	$64,198	$82,125	$105,000	$89,048
301+ People	195	$64,000	$79,084	$100,000	$89,396

United States

Total Compensation Based on Exchange Rate

	N	25th Percentile	Median	75th Percentile	Mean
1 - 10 People	111	$63,500	$77,500	$98,400	$89,835
11 - 25 People	83	$67,500	$82,000	$93,777	$85,661
26 - 50 People	82	$65,000	$80,000	$99,500	$91,531
51 - 100 People	75	$70,200	$85,400	$99,000	$89,945
101 - 300 People	68	$70,000	$87,000	$104,500	$94,514
301+ People	108	$70,050	$85,000	$104,000	$90,318

Total Compensation Based on OECD PPP

	N	25th Percentile	Median	75th Percentile	Mean
1 - 10 People	111	$63,500	$77,500	$98,400	$89,835
11 - 25 People	83	$67,500	$82,000	$93,777	$85,661
26 - 50 People	82	$65,000	$80,000	$99,500	$91,531
51 - 100 People	75	$70,200	$85,400	$99,000	$89,945
101 - 300 People	68	$70,000	$87,000	$104,500	$94,514
301+ People	108	$70,050	$85,000	$104,000	$90,318

Compensation by Number of People in Project Management in Organization

Canada

Total Compensation Based on Exchange Rate

	N	25th Percentile	Median	75th Percentile	Mean
1 - 10 People	32	$35,632	$49,090	$80,289	$70,844
11 - 300 People	72	$45,365	$52,268	$63,367	$61,280
301+ People	23	$44,689	$56,877	$62,394	$54,962

Total Compensation Based on OECD PPP

	N	25th Percentile	Median	75th Percentile	Mean
1 - 10 People	32	$44,978	$60,470	$88,000	$81,272
11 - 300 People	72	$51,561	$63,889	$75,214	$68,231
301+ People	23	$55,556	$67,949	$73,333	$66,138

Asia

Total Compensation Based on Exchange Rate

	N	25th Percentile	Median	75th Percentile	Mean
1 - 10 People	--	--	--	--	--
11 - 300 People	36	$33,250	$84,197	$114,200	$80,498
301+ People	22	$62,348	$103,000	$131,500	$111,094

Total Compensation Based on OECD PPP

	N	25th Percentile	Median	75th Percentile	Mean
1 - 10 People	--	--	--	--	--
11 - 300 People	36	$43,119	$78,056	$109,822	$80,808
301+ People	22	$60,875	$96,689	$121,500	$100,234

Australia/New Zealand

Total Compensation Based on Exchange Rate

	N	25th Percentile	Median	75th Percentile	Mean
1 - 10 People	14	$43,379	$50,300	$43,705	$52,728
11 - 300 People	25	$39,559	$46,296	$82,032	$57,579
301+ People	13	$44,333	$61,000	$81,056	$63,974

Total Compensation Based on OECD PPP

	N	25th Percentile	Median	75th Percentile	Mean
1 - 10 People	14	$50,450	$59,160	$69,557	$62,566
11 - 300 People	25	$47,710	$59,121	$111,718	$71,678
301+ People	13	$58,552	$80,534	$92,091	$78,641

Compensation by Number of People in Project Management in Organization

Europe

Total Compensation Based on Exchange Rate

	N	25th Percentile	Median	75th Percentile	Mean
1 - 10 People	11	$35,000	$47,200	$86,720	$68,566
11 - 300 People	33	$50,464	$60,319	$76,291	$70,305
301+ People	17	$47,722	$88,682	$118,500	$86,703

Total Compensation Based on OECD PPP

	N	25th Percentile	Median	75th Percentile	Mean
1 - 10 People	11	$40,000	$47,704	$87,349	$71,148
11 - 300 People	33	$50,151	$64,250	$90,558	$73,305
301+ People	17	$87,346	$45,064	$90,361	$87,346

Latin America

Total Compensation Based on Exchange Rate

	N	25th Percentile	Median	75th Percentile	Mean
1 - 10 People	--	--	--	--	--
11 - 300 People	26	$37,875	$68,336	$85,700	$71,340
301+ People	--	--	--	--	--

Total Compensation Based on OECD PPP

	N	25th Percentile	Median	75th Percentile	Mean
1 - 10 People	--	--	--	--	--
11 - 300 People	26	$41,650	$70,913	$90,850	$77,089
301+ People	--	--	--	--	--

Middle East

Total Compensation Based on Exchange Rate

	N	25th Percentile	Median	75th Percentile	Mean
1 - 10 People	--	--	--	--	--
11 - 300 People	13	$30,350	$60,000	$79,890	$62,151
301+ People	--	--	--	--	--

Total Compensation Based on OECD PPP

	N	25th Percentile	Median	75th Percentile	Mean
1 - 10 People	--	--	--	--	--
11 - 300 People	11	$40,000	$67,000	$98,000	$74,364
301+ People	--	--	--	--	--

Compensation by Number of Employees at Location

For the most part, there was a uniform distribution on a global basis between the number of employees at respondents' locations and their mean total compensation. The one exception was for respondents who had between 500 and 1,000 employees at their locations. Mean total compensation for these individuals was much higher ($95,930) than for respondents who had fewer or more employees at their locations.

Within the United States, there was no clear correlation between mean total compensation and number of employees at respondents' locations. Respondents who had fewer employees at their locations actually had higher mean total compensation. Only in Asia was there a direct and strong correlation between mean total compensation and number of employees at PMI respondents' locations.

Compensation by Number of Employees at Location

Global

Total Compensation Based on Exchange Rate

	N	25th Percentile	Median	75th Percentile	Mean
1 - 10 People	116	$52,130	$76,500	$100,000	$84,802
11 - 20 People	74	$52,238	$73,500	$95,500	$85,339
21 - 50 People	168	$50,372	$70,500	$96,224	$82,419
51 - 100 People	150	$54,000	$76,000	$94,200	$80,230
101 - 200 People	171	$56,600	$75,000	$97,700	$80,415
201 - 500 People	176	$56,000	$71,547	$95,000	$80,341
501 - 1,000 People	88	$53,483	$77,250	$95,750	$95,930
1,001+ People	153	$61,457	$76,083	$92,888	$78,984

Total Compensation Based on OECD PPP

	N	25th Percentile	Median	75th Percentile	Mean
1 - 10 People	116	$57,939	$77,056	$103,200	$90,163
11 - 20 People	74	$61,359	$72,325	$97,250	$87,420
21 - 50 People	166	$55,000	$72,284	$96,333	$84,448
51 - 100 People	150	$58,779	$76,000	$95,250	$82,747
101 - 200 People	170	$61,845	$76,068	$96,800	$82,492
201 - 500 People	174	$60,000	$74,329	$95,361	$83,510
501 - 1,000 People	88	$59,925	$79,743	$96,000	$97,344
1,001+ People	153	$64,884	$76,923	$92,888	$80,482

United States

Total Compensation Based on Exchange Rate

	N	25th Percentile	Median	75th Percentile	Mean
1 - 10 People	65	$64,900	$85,000	$108,500	$94,908
11 - 20 People	45	$68,650	$85,000	$104,000	$102,963
21 - 50 People	79	$63,000	$77,000	$94,000	$88,170
51 - 100 People	96	$66,100	$82,750	$98,300	$85,838
101 - 200 People	98	$67,875	$83,000	$100,000	$87,584
201 - 500 People	112	$63,875	$79,500	$99,500	$83,923
501 - 1,000 People	46	$70,575	$84,000	$95,250	$86,253
1,001+ People	110	$68,659	$80,500	$95,050	$84,784

Total Compensation Based on OECD PPP

	N	25th Percentile	Median	75th Percentile	Mean
1 - 10 People	65	$64,900	$85,000	$108,500	$94,908
11 - 20 People	45	$68,650	$85,000	$104,000	$102,963
21 - 50 People	79	$63,000	$77,000	$94,000	$88,170
51 - 100 People	96	$66,100	$82,750	$98,300	$85,838
101 - 200 People	98	$67,875	$83,000	$100,000	$87,584
201 - 500 People	112	$63,875	$79,500	$99,500	$83,923
501 - 1,000 People	46	$70,575	$84,000	$95,250	$86,253
1,001+ People	110	$68,659	$80,500	$95,050	$84,784

Compensation by Number of Employees at Location

Canada

Total Compensation Based on Exchange Rate

	N	25th Percentile	Median	75th Percentile	Mean
1 - 30 People	34	$40,426	$52,396	$80,500	$71,615
31 - 599 People	93	$43,680	$52,814	$63,573	$58,072
600+ People	32	$38,180	$50,613	$57,215	$53,508

Total Compensation Based on OECD PPP

	N	25th Percentile	Median	75th Percentile	Mean
1 - 30 People	34	$50,961	$64,316	$85,218	$80,393
31 - 599 People	93	$51,141	$64,000	$75,214	$68,882
600+ People	32	$43,621	$61,325	$72,562	$63,283

Asia

Total Compensation Based on Exchange Rate

	N	25th Percentile	Median	75th Percentile	Mean
1 - 30 People	11	$30,000	$89,856	$100,000	$75,581
31 - 599 People	46	$65,226	$98,221	$125,250	$107,771
600+ People	19	$62,500	$94,000	$110,000	$157,120

Total Compensation Based on OECD PPP

	N	25th Percentile	Median	75th Percentile	Mean
1 - 30 People	11	$30,000	$76,112	$100,000	$72,470
31 - 599 People	46	$63,533	$80,000	$112,500	$101,260
600+ People	19	$49,742	$75,000	$106,000	$150,280

Australia/New Zealand

Total Compensation Based on Exchange Rate

	N	25th Percentile	Median	75th Percentile	Mean
1 - 30 People	19	$40,000	$50,000	$52,938	$67,136
31 - 599 People	38	$39,340	$49,998	$70,440	$56,266
600+ People	--	--	--	--	--

Total Compensation Based on OECD PPP

	N	25th Percentile	Median	75th Percentile	Mean
1 - 30 People	19	$50,000	$53,435	$68,702	$80,701
31 - 599 People	38	$49,618	$63,256	$92,057	$69,933
600+ People	--	--	--	--	--

Compensation by Number of Employees at Location

Europe

Total Compensation Based on Exchange Rate

	N	25th Percentile	Median	75th Percentile	Mean
1 - 30 People	12	$32,225	$58,777	$106,890	$67,090
31 - 599 People	39	$52,000	$61,500	$94,800	$76,131
600+ People	14	$36,011	$61,472	$80,966	$66,205

Total Compensation Based on OECD PPP

	N	25th Percentile	Median	75th Percentile	Mean
1 - 30 People	12	$30,901	$50,000	$107,500	$65,373
31 - 599 People	39	$51,356	$64,250	$100,000	$77,850
600+ People	14	$41,268	$70,396	$95,250	$73,985

Latin America

Total Compensation Based on Exchange Rate

	N	25th Percentile	Median	75th Percentile	Mean
1 - 30 People	13	$22,716	$44,400	$98,000	$67,209
31 - 599 People	25	$37,750	$66,672	$80,500	$90,103
600+ People	--	--	--	--	--

Total Compensation Based on OECD PPP

	N	25th Percentile	Median	75th Percentile	Mean
1 - 30 People	13	$29,071	$48,000	$98,000	$69,887
31 - 599 People	25	$39,300	$70,000	$84,400	$94,360
600+ People	--	--	--	--	--

Middle East

Total Compensation Based on Exchange Rate

	N	25th Percentile	Median	75th Percentile	Mean
1 - 30 People	--	--	--	--	--
31 - 599 People	19	$31,216	$65,000	$98,000	$72,227
600+ People	--	--	--	--	--

Total Compensation Based on OECD PPP

	N	25th Percentile	Median	75th Percentile	Mean
1 - 30 People	--	--	--	--	--
31 - 599 People	14	$39,479	$76,230	$133,058	$82,218
600+ People	--	--	--	--	--

Compensation by Number of Employees in Organization

On a global basis, the relationship between mean total compensation and number of employees in respondents' organizations was U-shaped with respondents whose organizations had relatively few or large numbers of employees within their organizations having the highest mean total compensation. For example, respondents whose organizations had fewer than 50 employees earned a mean of $91,595 in total compensation. Respondents whose firms had over 20,000 employees averaged $92,215 in total compensation.

Within the United States, respondents whose organizations had fewer than 50 employees had the highest mean total compensation ($116,272). Among firms with more than 50 employees, mean total compensation was unaffected regardless of the number of employees. Asia was the only region of the world where there was a direct relationship between mean total compensation and number of employees in respondents' organizations.

Compensation by Number of Employees in Organization

Global

Total Compensation Based on Exchange Rate

	N	25th Percentile	Median	75th Percentile	Mean
1 - 50 People	111	$51,964	$75,640	$105,060	$91,595
51 - 100 People	61	$43,006	$71,000	$94,500	$73,528
101 - 200 People	59	$54,000	$77,000	$100,000	$80,992
201 - 500 People	146	$55,075	$70,500	$90,000	$77,382
501 - 1,000 People	69	$45,750	$67,500	$90,000	$79,704
1,001 - 5,000 People	232	$52,575	$71,500	$91,417	$79,807
5,001 - 10,000 People	104	$52,860	$68,000	$90,000	$79,787
10,001 - 20,000 People	72	$61,982	$80,000	$105,750	$84,762
20,001+ People	183	$62,394	$80,000	$100,000	$92,215

Total Compensation Based on OECD PPP

	N	25th Percentile	Median	75th Percentile	Mean
1 - 50 People	111	$57,200	$80,000	$110,000	$96,373
51 - 100 People	61	$51,141	$71,000	$94,500	$75,696
101 - 200 People	59	$55,000	$78,000	$100,000	$83,978
201 - 500 People	145	$60,970	$72,000	$90,000	$79,966
501 - 1,000 People	68	$48,050	$71,413	$105,000	$82,149
1,001 - 5,000 People	230	$60,129	$75,000	$91,598	$83,755
5,001 - 10,000 People	104	$57,493	$70,361	$89,936	$79,713
10,001 - 20,000 People	71	$66,000	$80,000	$105,000	$83,757
20,001+ People	183	$67,468	$82,500	$102,000	$94,389

Compensation by Number of Employees in Organization

United States

Total Compensation Based on Exchange Rate

	N	25th Percentile	Median	75th Percentile	Mean
1 - 50 People	43	$70,000	$85,000	$107,000	$116,272
51 - 100 People	39	$69,000	$76,000	$98,400	$86,917
101 - 200 People	37	$70,500	$89,500	$108,500	$88,682
201 - 500 People	85	$65,000	$73,000	$94,917	$85,306
501 - 1,000 People	43	$54,000	$80,000	$90,000	$82,764
1,001 - 5,000 People	130	$68,225	$80,000	$96,687	$84,220
5,001 - 10,000 People	64	$67,275	$80,000	$93,944	$90,133
10,001 - 20,000 People	45	$64,000	$80,000	$105,500	$85,652
20,001+ People	129	$69,500	$85,000	$103,500	$89,755

Total Compensation Based on OECD PPP

	N	25th Percentile	Median	75th Percentile	Mean
1 - 50 People	43	$70,000	$85,000	$107,000	$116,272
51 - 100 People	39	$69,000	$76,000	$98,400	$86,917
101 - 200 People	37	$70,500	$89,500	$108,500	$88,682
201 - 500 People	85	$65,000	$73,000	$94,917	$85,306
501 - 1,000 People	43	$54,000	$80,000	$90,000	$82,764
1,001 - 5,000 People	130	$68,225	$80,000	$96,687	$84,220
5,001 - 10,000 People	64	$67,275	$80,000	$93,944	$90,133
10,001 - 20,000 People	45	$64,000	$80,000	$105,500	$85,652
20,001+ People	129	$69,500	$85,000	$103,500	$89,755

Compensation by Number of Employees in Organization

Canada

Total Compensation Based on Exchange Rate

	N	25th Percentile	Median	75th Percentile	Mean
1 - 200 People	36	$38,290	$51,568	$81,185	$71,018
201 - 14,999 People	90	$44,357	$52,238	$59,587	$58,785
15,000+ People	27	$44,012	$57,554	$74,482	$62,354

Total Compensation Based on OECD PPP

	N	25th Percentile	Median	75th Percentile	Mean
1 - 200 People	36	$48,333	$54,278	$91,654	$79,385
201 - 14,999 People	90	$51,061	$64,000	$72,650	$66,397
15,000+ People	27	$55,556	$72,650	$89,744	$74,635

Asia

Total Compensation Based on Exchange Rate

	N	25th Percentile	Median	75th Percentile	Mean
1 - 200 People	14	$29,500	$80,656	$120,750	$81,795
201 - 14,999 People	48	$61,919	$90,953	$115,543	$102,012
15,000+ People	--	--	--	--	--

Total Compensation Based on OECD PPP

	N	25th Percentile	Median	75th Percentile	Mean
1 - 200 People	14	$31,352	$69,767	$116,700	$73,116
201 - 14,999 People	48	$58,250	$76,235	$108,467	$98,888
15,000+ People	--	--	--	--	--

Australia/New Zealand

Total Compensation Based on Exchange Rate

	N	25th Percentile	Median	75th Percentile	Mean
1 - 200 People	19	$38,233	$50,000	$52,000	$51,461
201 - 14,999 People	30	$39,927	$49,998	$68,499	$56,550
15,000+ People	--	--	--	--	--

Total Compensation Based on OECD PPP

	N	25th Percentile	Median	75th Percentile	Mean
1 - 200 People	19	$49,324	$52,000	$74,234	$62,698
201 - 14,999 People	30	$50,000	$64,199	$87,840	$70,696
15,000+ People	--	--	--	--	--

Compensation by Number of Employees in Organization

Europe

Total Compensation Based on Exchange Rate

	N	25th Percentile	Median	75th Percentile	Mean
1 - 200 People	14	$45,400	$92,140	$120,000	$83,981
201 - 14,999 People	37	$40,958	$53,000	$70,000	$63,230
15,000+ People	15	$61,500	$73,170	$103,264	$85,517

Total Compensation Based on OECD PPP

	N	25th Percentile	Median	75th Percentile	Mean
1 - 200 People	14	$45,400	$93,674	$120,000	$85,342
201 - 14,999 People	37	$42,750	$53,000	$70,261	$65,938
15,000+ People	15	$61,500	$81,116	$103,264	$87,079

Latin America

Total Compensation Based on Exchange Rate

	N	25th Percentile	Median	75th Percentile	Mean
1 - 200 People	14	$31,750	$68,336	$97,000	$73,035
201 - 14,999 People	24	$38,275	$60,259	$80,000	$88,395
15,000+ People	--	--	--	--	--

Total Compensation Based on OECD PPP

	N	25th Percentile	Median	75th Percentile	Mean
1 - 200 People	14	$33,286	$75,000	$105,000	$80,391
201 - 14,999 People	24	$40,950	$66,259	$80,000	$90,862
15,000+ People	--	--	--	--	--

Middle East

Total Compensation Based on Exchange Rate

	N	25th Percentile	Median	75th Percentile	Mean
1 - 200 People	--	--	--	--	--
201 - 14,999 People	20	$38,438	$76,230	$99,500	$76,051
15,000+ People	--	--	--	--	--

Total Compensation Based on OECD PPP

	N	25th Percentile	Median	75th Percentile	Mean
1 - 200 People	--	--	--	--	--
201 - 14,999 People	15	$41,700	$86,000	$133,000	$86,650
15,000+ People	--	--	--	--	--

Compensation by Number of Years in Project Management

Global figures (see page 117) show a strong correlation between mean total compensation and number of years in project management. Respondents with only 1 or 2 years of experience in project management had a mean total compensation of $65,508, while mean total compensation grew steadily to $112,005 for respondents with more than 20 years of experience. Each year of additional experience in project management corresponded to approximately $2,300 more in mean total compensation and approximately $1,600 more in median total compensation.

The correlation within the United States between mean total compensation and number of years in project management was also strong. Respondents with only 1 or 2 years of experience earned only $65,620 in mean total compensation, while their counterparts with over 20 years of experience had a mean total compensation of $115,109. Each additional year of experience in project management for United States respondents resulted in approximately $2,500 more in mean total compensation and approximately $1,700 more in median total compensation.

The strong and direct correlation between number of years in project management and mean total compensation held for other parts of the world as well. For example, Canadian respondents with fewer than 5 years of experience had a mean total compensation of $46,681, while their more experienced colleagues (15+ years) earned $68,985 in mean total compensation. Figures for Europe showed an even more dramatic increase in mean total compensation as respondents' years of experience increased.

Compensation by Number of Years in Project Management

Global

Total Compensation Based on Exchange Rate

	N	25th Percentile	Median	75th Percentile	Mean
1 - 2 Years	79	$38,000	$52,814	$72,000	$65,508
3 - 5 Years	262	$46,540	$65,000	$82,625	$66,804
6 - 10 Years	353	$56,000	$75,000	$97,026	$81,228
11 - 15 Years	232	$62,545	$80,000	$100,000	$85,914
16 - 20 Years	141	$67,500	$85,999	$105,500	$98,150
21+ Years	107	$67,000	$86,000	$112,500	$112,005

Total Compensation Based on OECD PPP

	N	25th Percentile	Median	75th Percentile	Mean
1 - 2 Years	79	$40,000	$57,432	$70,500	$64,240
3 - 5 Years	262	$50,320	$66,250	$85,000	$69,510
6 - 10 Years	351	$60,811	$77,000	$98,400	$84,617
11 - 15 Years	230	$68,468	$80,267	$100,000	$88,389
16 - 20 Years	141	$69,500	$86,000	$105,590	$99,773
21+ Years	107	$70,000	$86,900	$115,000	$114,839

United States

Total Compensation Based on Exchange Rate

	N	25th Percentile	Median	75th Percentile	Mean
1 - 2 Years	51	$47,800	$64,500	$79,000	$65,620
3 - 5 Years	174	$59,875	$73,395	$90,000	$76,184
6 - 10 Years	205	$67,500	$82,500	$99,900	$88,040
11 - 15 Years	130	$75,000	$96,500	$100,750	$91,750
16 - 20 Years	83	$74,500	$88,300	$106,000	$101,860
21+ Years	59	$80,000	$99,000	$135,000	$115,109

Total Compensation Based on OECD PPP

	N	25th Percentile	Median	75th Percentile	Mean
1 - 2 Years	51	$47,800	$64,500	$79,000	$65,620
3 - 5 Years	174	$59,875	$73,395	$90,000	$76,184
6 - 10 Years	205	$67,500	$82,500	$99,900	$88,040
11 - 15 Years	130	$75,000	$96,500	$100,750	$91,750
16 - 20 Years	83	$74,500	$88,300	$106,000	$101,860
21+ Years	59	$80,000	$99,000	$135,000	$115,109

Compensation by Number of Years in Project Management

Canada

Total Compensation Based on Exchange Rate

	N	25th Percentile	Median	75th Percentile	Mean
1 – 4 Years	32	$31,908	$36,936	$47,227	$46,681
5 - 15 Years	97	$47,397	$57,554	$71,095	$64,850
16+ Years	32	$45,366	$55,179	$76,258	$68,985

Total Compensation Based on OECD PPP

	N	25th Percentile	Median	75th Percentile	Mean
1 - 4 Years	32	$36,923	$44,444	$53,165	$46,051
5 - 15 Years	97	$56,837	$68,376	$76,931	$75,858
16+ Years	32	$51,070	$69,658	$93,013	$79,542

Asia

Total Compensation Based on Exchange Rate

	N	25th Percentile	Median	75th Percentile	Mean
1 - 4 Years	--	--	--	--	--
5 - 15 Years	56	$63,450	$95,500	$119,059	$93,100
16+ Years	19	$76,000	$89,856	$125,000	$174,247

Total Compensation Based on OECD PPP

	N	25th Percentile	Median	75th Percentile	Mean
1 - 4 Years	--	--	--	--	--
5 - 15 Years	56	$62,125	$80,000	$105,897	$86,148
16+ Years	19	$74,534	$80,000	$106,000	$166,596

Australia/New Zealand

Total Compensation Based on Exchange Rate

	N	25th Percentile	Median	75th Percentile	Mean
1 - 4 Years	43	$42,437	$50,600	$69,408	$65,848
5 - 15 Years	15	$46,296	$63,000	$91,171	$69,888
16+ Years	--	--	--	--	--

Total Compensation Based on OECD PPP

	N	25th Percentile	Median	75th Percentile	Mean
1 - 4 Years	43	$50,000	$62,162	$81,186	$82,031
5 - 15 Years	15	$53,435	$67,000	$108,396	$81,879
16+ Years	--	--	--	--	--

Compensation by Number of Years in Project Management

Europe

Total Compensation Based on Exchange Rate

	N	25th Percentile	Median	75th Percentile	Mean
1 - 4 Years	12	$34,167	$42,164	$67,534	$49,074
5 - 15 Years	45	$48,064	$60,570	$93,270	$74,477
16+ Years	16	$65,437	$85,860	$117,500	$88,556

Total Compensation Based on OECD PPP

	N	25th Percentile	Median	75th Percentile	Mean
1 - 4 Years	12	$37,247	$43,520	$68,492	$50,443
5 - 15 Years	45	$47,414	$61,500	$96,154	$74,685
16+ Years	16	$69,250	$95,603	$120,000	$96,151

Latin America

Total Compensation Based on Exchange Rate

	N	25th Percentile	Median	75th Percentile	Mean
1 - 4 Years	--	--	--	--	--
5 - 15 Years	28	$35,125	$54,443	$85,850	$68,243
16+ Years	13	$62,000	$80,000	$98,000	$130,485

Total Compensation Based on OECD PPP

	N	25th Percentile	Median	75th Percentile	Mean
1 - 4 Years	--	--	--	--	--
5 - 15 Years	28	$36,000	$60,259	$93,950	$73,245
16+ Years	13	$62,000	$80,000	$98,000	$130,485

Middle East

Total Compensation Based on Exchange Rate

	N	25th Percentile	Median	75th Percentile	Mean
1 - 4 Years	--	--	--	--	--
5 - 15 Years	13	$32,955	$60,000	$96,144	$64,896
16+ Years	11	$50,000	$77,460	$100,000	$81,651

Total Compensation Based on OECD PPP

	N	25th Percentile	Median	75th Percentile	Mean
1 - 4 Years	--	--	--	--	--
5 - 15 Years	--	--	--	--	--
16+ Years	11	$50,000	$77,460	$100,000	$81,651

Mean Total Compensation by Number of Years Worked for Current Employer

On a global basis, years with one's current employer had little impact on mean total compensation through the first 15 years of employment. First-year employees had a mean total compensation of $77,341. Figures varied slightly as respondents' years of experience with their employers increased to 15 years (mean total compensation for respondents with 11 to 15 years of experience was $75,267). After 15 years of experience, mean total compensation rose dramatically with respondents who had 16 to 20 years of experience earning $89,383 in mean total compensation, and respondents with over 20 years of experience with their employers earning $101,455 in mean total compensation.

Figures for the United States were similar to global figures in overall pattern, yet the increases after 15 years of experience were not as dramatic. As respondents went from 11 to 15 years of experience to 16 to 20 years of experience with the same employer, mean total compensation grew from $83,440 to $88,598. Mean total compensation increased to $93,105 after 20 years of experience with the same employer.

Respondents in Asia, Europe, and Latin America experienced significant increases in mean total compensation as their experience with a given employer increased. Figures for Canada and Australia/New Zealand did not show a discernable correlation between mean total compensation and years with one's employer.

Mean Total Compensation by Number of Years Worked for Current Employer

Global

Total Compensation Based on Exchange Rate

	N	25th Percentile	Median	75th Percentile	Mean
1 Year	205	$59,100	$74,113	$91,500	$77,341
2 Years	141	$50,300	$71,000	$91,750	$77,354
3 - 5 Years	248	$46,775	$70,000	$91,070	$79,673
6 - 10 Years	175	$49,000	$73,170	$96,000	$78,298
11 - 15 Years	133	$55,050	$98,500	$88,659	$75,267
16 - 20 Years	114	$60,600	$79,050	$98,100	$89,383
21+ Years	153	$68,509	$88,000	$104,989	$101,455

Total Compensation Based on OECD PPP

	N	25th Percentile	Median	75th Percentile	Mean
1 Year	205	$61,250	$76,000	$95,000	$80,494
2 Years	140	$56,124	$74,200	$93,097	$79,118
3 - 5 Years	245	$54,500	$74,500	$91,800	$83,825
6 - 10 Years	175	$51,500	$75,000	$97,000	$81,307
11 - 15 Years	133	$56,855	$71,000	$88,750	$76,070
16 - 20 Years	113	$65,400	$80,000	$99,200	$92,625
21+ Years	153	$68,323	$85,000	$104,000	$100,448

United States

Total Compensation Based on Exchange Rate

	N	25th Percentile	Median	75th Percentile	Mean
1 Year	142	$65,900	$80,750	$98,100	$83,877
2 Years	83	$63,000	$78,375	$96,500	$84,268
3 - 5 Years	155	$65,000	$80,580	$100,000	$82,286
6 - 10 Years	97	$63,250	$85,400	$100,000	$87,440
11 - 15 Years	79	$64,000	$75,659	$90,000	$83,440
16 - 20 Years	64	$69,250	$81,000	$97,875	$88,598
21+ Years	82	$70,000	$89,000	$100,250	$93,105

Total Compensation Based on OECD PPP

	N	25th Percentile	Median	75th Percentile	Mean
1 Year	142	$65,900	$80,750	$98,100	$83,877
2 Years	83	$63,000	$78,375	$96,500	$84,268
3 - 5 Years	155	$65,000	$80,580	$100,000	$82,286
6 - 10 Years	97	$63,250	$85,400	$100,000	$87,440
11 - 15 Years	79	$64,000	$75,659	$90,000	$83,440
16 - 20 Years	64	$69,250	$81,000	$97,875	$88,598
21+ Years	82	$70,000	$89,000	$100,250	$93,105

Mean Total Compensation by Number of Years Worked for Current Employer

Canada

Total Compensation Based on Exchange Rate

	N	25th Percentile	Median	75th Percentile	Mean
1 Year	31	$40,626	$52,400	$64,324	$54,292
2 - 14 Years	89	$39,854	$51,676	$61,667	$63,908
15+ Years	39	$46,720	$54,000	$71,095	$59,976

Total Compensation Based on OECD PPP

	N	25th Percentile	Median	75th Percentile	Mean
1 Year	31	$50,000	$60,000	$78,000	$65,300
2 - 14 Years	89	$47,436	$63,675	$74,180	$71,363
15+ Years	39	$54,000	$64,000	$75,214	$68,649

Asia

Total Compensation Based on Exchange Rate

	N	25th Percentile	Median	75th Percentile	Mean
1 Year	--	--	--	--	--
2 - 14 Years	29	$11,794	$48,500	$89,698	$72,813
15+ Years	49	$85,000	$104,005	$124,000	$136,805

Total Compensation Based on OECD PPP

	N	25th Percentile	Median	75th Percentile	Mean
1 Year	--	--	--	--	--
2 - 14 Years	29	$40,953	$57,377	$98,000	$81,724
15+ Years	49	$70,817	$89,856	$115,000	$124,717

Australia/New Zealand

Total Compensation Based on Exchange Rate

	N	25th Percentile	Median	75th Percentile	Mean
1 Year	13	$39,117	$51,762	$80,808	$60,834
2 - 14 Years	44	$40,039	$50,000	$67,390	$54,706
15+ Years	11	$40,000	$50,000	$91,171	$64,870

Total Compensation Based on OECD PPP

	N	25th Percentile	Median	75th Percentile	Mean
1 Year	13	$49,471	$70,000	$110,670	$79,531
2 - 14 Years	44	$49,714	$61,616	$85,405	$67,354
15+ Years	11	$51,185	$64,885	$100,000	$77,388

Mean Total Compensation by Number of Years Worked for Current Employer

Europe

Total Compensation Based on Exchange Rate

	N	25th Percentile	Median	75th Percentile	Mean
1 Year	--	--	--	--	--
2 - 14 Years	49	$41,878	$61,500	$90,211	$70,019
15+ Years	14	$49,604	$70,000	$132,250	$89,017

Total Compensation Based on OECD PPP

	N	25th Percentile	Median	75th Percentile	Mean
1 Year	--	--	--	--	--
2 - 14 Years	49	$42,463	$61,500	$91,335	$70,840
15+ Years	14	$51,676	$85,000	$147,427	$95,596

Latin America

Total Compensation Based on Exchange Rate

	N	25th Percentile	Median	75th Percentile	Mean
1 Year	--	--	--	--	--
2 - 14 Years	31	$25,002	$42,000	$85,000	$58,765
15+ Years	15	$54,000	$72,000	$81,000	$121,065

Total Compensation Based on OECD PPP

	N	25th Percentile	Median	75th Percentile	Mean
1 Year	--	--	--	--	--
2 - 14 Years	31	$31,142	$48,000	$85,000	$61,798
15+ Years	15	$54,000	$74,300	$120,000	$125,609

Middle East

Total Compensation Based on Exchange Rate

	N	25th Percentile	Median	75th Percentile	Mean
1 Year	--	--	--	--	--
2 - 14 Years	19	$37,917	$65,000	$95,843	$68,437
15+ Years	--	--	--	--	--

Total Compensation Based on OECD PPP

	N	25th Percentile	Median	75th Percentile	Mean
1 Year	--	--	--	--	--
2 - 14 Years	15	$50,000	66,000	$96,444	$74,768
15+ Years	--	--	--	--	--

Compensation by PMP Certification

Tables on pages 125 through 127 show total compensation for respondents who have earned the Project Management Professional (PMP) Certification versus those who have not. On a global basis, the PMP Certification resulted in a $5,000 mean total compensation differential. That is, PMPs earned approximately 6% more than those who have not earned the certification.

Within the United States, the differential in mean total compensation between those who have and those who have not earned the PMP Certification was greater ($9,000). PMPs earned 10% more in mean total compensation within the United States.

PMP Certification resulted in positive differentials in total compensation. Below are percentages that reflect how much greater mean total compensation is for respondents who have earned the PMP Certification:

26% - Canada
2% - Asia
31% - Australia/New Zealand
10% - Europe
14% - Middle East

Compensation by PMP Certification

Global

Total Compensation Based on Exchange Rate

	N	25th Percentile	Median	75th Percentile	Mean
PMP	426	$58,473	$80,000	$100,000	$85,558
Non PMP	727	$52,205	$71,000	$93,900	$80,413

Total Compensation Based on OECD PPP

	N	25th Percentile	Median	75th Percentile	Mean
PMP	424	$65,854	$81,000	$100,750	$89,522
Non PMP	724	$57,265	$72,250	$94,000	$82,208

United States

Total Compensation Based on Exchange Rate

	N	25th Percentile	Median	75th Percentile	Mean
PMP	224	$74,125	$86,950	$102,625	$93,792
Non PMP	452	$63,125	$79,100	$97,875	$84,881

Total Compensation Based on OECD PPP

	N	25th Percentile	Median	75th Percentile	Mean
PMP	224	$74,089	$86,700	$101,375	$93,535
Non PMP	452	$63,125	$79,100	$97,875	$84,994

Canada

Total Compensation Based on Exchange Rate

	N	25th Percentile	Median	75th Percentile	Mean
PMP	59	$51,000	$57,554	$72,300	$71,162
Non PMP	105	$39,678	$49,428	$59,792	$56,398

Total Compensation Based on OECD PPP

	N	25th Percentile	Median	75th Percentile	Mean
PMP	59	$55,556	$72,650	$89,744	$82,556
Non PMP	105	$47,009	$59,830	$72,575	$63,512

Compensation by PMP Certification

Asia

Total Compensation Based on Exchange Rate

	N	25th Percentile	Median	75th Percentile	Mean
PMP	42	$65,888	$89,500	$113,995	$91,132
Non PMP	40	$57,473	$90,953	$123,750	$88,964

Total Compensation Based on OECD PPP

	N	25th Percentile	Median	75th Percentile	Mean
PMP	42	$57,282	$78,179	$105,692	$87,170
Non PMP	40	$54,062	$80,000	$105,898	$83,010

Australia/New Zealand

Total Compensation Based on Exchange Rate

	N	25th Percentile	Median	75th Percentile	Mean
PMP	38	$43,205	$51,881	$76,760	$69,950
Non PMP	33	$39,704	$46,296	$65,499	$53,563

Total Compensation Based on OECD PPP

	N	25th Percentile	Median	75th Percentile	Mean
PMP	38	$51,300	$65,942	$93,893	$86,515
Non PMP	33	$49,471	$60,000	$77,117	$67,160

Europe

Total Compensation Based on Exchange Rate

	N	25th Percentile	Median	75th Percentile	Mean
PMP	29	$52,400	$69,000	$101,632	$77,929
Non PMP	43	$40,000	$60,555	$91,740	$70,635

Total Compensation Based on OECD PPP

	N	25th Percentile	Median	75th Percentile	Mean
PMP	29	$52,400	$70,000	$101,632	$79,015
Non PMP	43	$40,000	$70,000	$100,000	$73,328

Compensation by PMP Certification

Latin America

Total Compensation Based on Exchange Rate

	N	25th Percentile	Median	75th Percentile	Mean
PMP	19	$42,000	$70,000	$81,000	$76,536
Non PMP	29	$27,501	$50,886	$86,400	$81,362

Total Compensation Based on OECD PPP

	N	25th Percentile	Median	75th Percentile	Mean
PMP	19	$42,000	$72,000	$100,000	$80,124
Non PMP	29	$33,595	$54,000	$86,400	$84,604

Middle East

Total Compensation Based on Exchange Rate

	N	25th Percentile	Median	75th Percentile	Mean
PMP	10	$29,346	$52,500	$136,000	$74,365
Non PMP	18	$39,479	$65,500	$95,993	$65,409

Total Compensation Based on OECD PPP

	N	25th Percentile	Median	75th Percentile	Mean
PMP	--	--	--	--	--
Non PMP	15	$40,000	$66,000	$96,444	$67,403

Compensation by Gender

Throughout the world there were significant differences in mean total compensation between male and female respondents. Globally, males' mean total compensation was 18% higher than females'. Percentage differentials between males' and females' mean total compensations within specific areas of the world are shown below:

16% - United States
29% - Canada
48% - Australia/New Zealand

Sufficient data were not available to make valid comparisons in other parts of the world.

Comparisons to 1996 [1]

Between 1996 and 2000, females had gained ground on males. In 1996, mean total compensation for males was 24% greater than their female counterparts. By 2000, this difference was reduced to 18%. Caution should be used in comparing 1996 data to 2000 data since the latter was a global study and the former included only Canada and the United States.

Compensation by Gender

Global

Total Compensation Based on Exchange Rate

	N	25th Percentile	Median	75th Percentile	Mean
Male	891	$57,554	$77,500	$98,000	$85,174
Female	293	$50,404	$68,718	$86,700	$71,895

Total Compensation Based on OECD PPP

	N	25th Percentile	Median	75th Percentile	Mean
Male	886	$61,529	$78,355	$100,000	$87,632
Female	293	$55,000	$70,000	$87,224	$74,514

United States

Total Compensation Based on Exchange Rate

	N	25th Percentile	Median	75th Percentile	Mean
Male	489	$69,650	$85,000	$101,750	$90,788
Female	218	$60,000	$74,900	$90,000	$78,402

Total Compensation Based on OECD PPP

	N	25th Percentile	Median	75th Percentile	Mean
Male	489	$69,650	$85,000	$101,750	$90,774
Female	218	$60,000	$74,900	$90,000	$78,402

Canada

Total Compensation Based on Exchange Rate

	N	25th Percentile	Median	75th Percentile	Mean
Male	127	$45,365	$53,830	$64,324	$64,185
Female	38	$34,864	$46,998	$57,554	$49,652

Total Compensation Based on OECD PPP

	N	25th Percentile	Median	75th Percentile	Mean
Male	127	$51,282	$65,812	$76,000	$71,922
Female	38	$44,017	$58,119	$72,650	$60,506

Compensation by Gender

Asia

Total Compensation Based on Exchange Rate

	N	25th Percentile	Median	75th Percentile	Mean
Male	81	$65,592	$95,000	$120,000	$114,692
Female	--	--	--	--	--

Total Compensation Based on OECD PPP

	N	25th Percentile	Median	75th Percentile	Mean
Male	81	$62,250	$80,000	$107,645	$109,698
Female	--	--	--	--	--

Australia/New Zealand

Total Compensation Based on Exchange Rate

	N	25th Percentile	Median	75th Percentile	Mean
Male	53	$42,476	$51,964	$76,738	$67,549
Female	17	$27,163	$40,000	$51,881	$45,518

Total Compensation Based on OECD PPP

	N	25th Percentile	Median	75th Percentile	Mean
Male	53	$51,359	$66,216	$90,888	$83,143
Female	17	$38,581	$49,618	$65,344	$59,067

Europe

Total Compensation Based on Exchange Rate

	N	25th Percentile	Median	75th Percentile	Mean
Male	66	$46,150	$62,875	$88,740	$71,339
Female	--	--	--	--	--

Total Compensation Based on OECD PPP

	N	25th Percentile	Median	75th Percentile	Mean
Male	66	$47,521	$69,500	$100,000	$73,579
Female	--	--	--	--	--

Compensation by Gender

Latin America

Total Compensation Based on Exchange Rate

	N	25th Percentile	Median	75th Percentile	Mean
Male	41	$34,500	$66,672	$90,500	$84,717
Female	--	--	--	--	--

Total Compensation Based on OECD PPP

	N	25th Percentile	Median	75th Percentile	Mean
Male	41	$36,500	$70,000	$96,000	$88,133
Female	--	--	--	--	--

Middle East

Total Compensation Based on Exchange Rate

	N	25th Percentile	Median	75th Percentile	Mean
Male	27	$40,000	$65,000	$96,444	$70,778
Female	--	--	--	--	--

Total Compensation Based on OECD PPP

	N	25th Percentile	Median	75th Percentile	Mean
Male	22	$47,925	$66,500	$98,500	$76,807
Female	--	--	--	--	--

Compensation by Age

On a global basis, age and mean total compensation were directly correlated with mean total compensation increasing at least $10,000 for each increase in age category (e.g., 35–44 was one age category; 45–54 was the next age category), as shown below.

Age Category	Mean Total Compensation
25 - 34 Years	$62,493
35 - 44 Years	$79,471
45 - 54 Years	$92,152
55 - 64 Years	$102,975

There was also a direct and strong correlation between age and mean total compensation for respondents within the United States, yet the figure for 35 to 44 year olds ($88,574) was not considerably less than the figure for 45 to 54 year olds ($92,930). In Canada, mean total compensation jumped considerably between the ages of 45 to 54 ($62,067) and 55 to 64 ($116,894), yet there were only 11 respondents in the latter age category. While other areas of the world lacked sufficient data to make complete comparisons between age and mean total compensation, for the most part there was a direct and strong correlation between these two factors around the globe, with Australia/New Zealand being the exception.

Compensation by Age

Global

Total Compensation Based on Exchange Rate

	N	25th Percentile	Median	75th Percentile	Mean
24 Years or less	--	--	--	--	--
25 - 34 Years	194	$38,231	$54,191	$75,000	$62,493
35 - 44 Years	495	$57,554	$75,000	$94,794	$79,471
45 - 54 Years	394	$63,375	$81,325	$101,875	$92,152
55 - 64 Years	89	$70,000	$88,000	$119,246	$102,975
65+ Years	--	--	--	--	--

Total Compensation Based on OECD PPP

	N	25th Percentile	Median	75th Percentile	Mean
24 Years or less	--	--	--	--	--
25 - 34 Years	194	$42,077	$56,546	$74,850	$64,572
35 - 44 Years	493	$60,000	$76,112	$96,000	$82,632
45 - 54 Years	392	$68,300	$81,450	$101,617	$94,335
55 - 64 Years	88	$70,000	$91,400	$120,000	$105,301
65+ Years	--	--	--	--	--

United States

Total Compensation Based on Exchange Rate

	N	25th Percentile	Median	75th Percentile	Mean
24 Years or less	--	--	--	--	--
25 - 34 Years	109	$48,700	$64,000	$80,540	$66,201
35 - 44 Years	297	$68,000	$82,000	$99,900	$88,574
45 - 54 Years	238	$71,000	$85,000	$101,125	$92,930
55 - 64 Years	56	$74,625	$91,900	$118,750	$107,551
65+ Years	--	--	--	--	--

Total Compensation Based on OECD PPP

	N	25th Percentile	Median	75th Percentile	Mean
24 Years or less	--	--	--	--	--
25 - 34 Years	109	$48,700	$64,000	$80,540	$66,201
35 - 44 Years	297	$68,000	$82,000	$99,400	$88,552
45 - 54 Years	238	$71,000	$85,000	$101,125	$92,930
55 - 64 Years	56	$74,625	$91,900	$118,750	$107,551
65+ Years	--	--	--	--	--

Compensation by Age

Canada

Total Compensation Based on Exchange Rate

	N	25th Percentile	Median	75th Percentile	Mean
24 Years or less	--	--	--	--	--
25 - 34 Years	32	$32,583	$40,204	$53,876	$52,689
35 - 44 Years	70	$44,008	$52,171	$60,939	$58,618
45 - 54 Years	50	$50,783	$57,554	$64,081	$62,067
55 - 64 Years	11	$57,554	$101,000	$162,000	$116,894
65+ Years	--	--	--	--	--

Total Compensation Based on OECD PPP

	N	25th Percentile	Median	75th Percentile	Mean
24 Years or less	--	--	--	--	--
25 - 34 Years	32	$40,277	$48,718	$65,277	$52,790
35 - 44 Years	70	$52,490	$60,769	$79,230	$69,736
45 - 54 Years	50	$62,714	$70,043	$75,410	$73,594
55 - 64 Years	11	$64,000	$101,000	$162,000	$124,334
65+ Years	--	--	--	--	--

Asia

Total Compensation Based on Exchange Rate

	N	25th Percentile	Median	75th Percentile	Mean
24 Years or less	--	--	--	--	--
25 - 34 Years	12	$9,733	$26,000	$61,125	$79,558
35 - 44 Years	28	$57,473	$78,000	$100,000	$77,057
45 - 54 Years	34	$94,262	$108,000	$127,000	$153,267
55 - 64 Years	--	--	--	--	--
65+ Years	--	--	--	--	--

Total Compensation Based on OECD PPP

	N	25th Percentile	Median	75th Percentile	Mean
24 Years or less	--	--	--	--	--
25 - 34 Years	12	$30,450	$43,320	$61,125	$86,478
35 - 44 Years	28	$54,062	$73,835	$97,000	$74,470
45 - 54 Years	34	$73,141	$100,000	$123,500	$142,727
55 - 64 Years	--	--	--	--	--
65+ Years	--	--	--	--	--

Compensation by Age

Australia/New Zealand

Total Compensation Based on Exchange Rate

	N	25th Percentile	Median	75th Percentile	Mean
24 Years or less	12	$28,758	$38,233	$44,169	$67,456
25 - 34 Years	29	$48,113	$51,964	$72,056	$59,845
35 - 44 Years	25	$40,587	$52,938	$70,584	$61,017
45 - 54 Years	--	--	--	--	--
55 - 64 Years	--	--	--	--	--
65+ Years	--	--	--	--	--

Total Compensation Based on OECD PPP

	N	25th Percentile	Median	75th Percentile	Mean
24 Years or less	12	$38,006	$49,618	$63,184	$89,444
25 - 34 Years	29	$50,300	$64,885	$87,514	$73,460
35 - 44 Years	25	$52,484	$66,216	$91,603	$75,508
45 - 54 Years	--	--	--	--	--
55 - 64 Years	--	--	--	--	--
65+ Years	--	--	--	--	--

Europe

Total Compensation Based on Exchange Rate

	N	25th Percentile	Median	75th Percentile	Mean
24 Years or less	--	--	--	--	--
25 - 34 Years	14	$26,400	$45,474	$62,602	$50,013
35 - 44 Years	32	$44,104	$64,689	$99,390	$77,511
45 - 54 Years	20	$58,209	$80,007	$116,250	$87,117
55 - 64 Years	--	--	--	--	--
65+ Years	--	--	--	--	--

Total Compensation Based on OECD PPP

	N	25th Percentile	Median	75th Percentile	Mean
24 Years or less	--	--	--	--	--
25 - 34 Years	14	$29,676	$42,912	$65,477	$50,412
35 - 44 Years	32	$45,261	$70,657	$100,000	$78,859
45 - 54 Years	20	$54,643	$80,321	$116,250	$85,621
55 - 64 Years	--	--	--	--	--
65+ Years	--	--	--	--	--

Compensation by Age

Latin America

Total Compensation Based on Exchange Rate

	N	25th Percentile	Median	75th Percentile	Mean
24 Years or less	--	--	--	--	--
25 - 34 Years	13	$16,608	$27,000	$62,200	$49,670
35 - 44 Years	18	$37,000	$66,258	$97,000	$70,506
45 - 54 Years	16	$54,000	$70,000	$93,250	$115,097
55 - 64 Years	--	--	--	--	--
65+ Years	--	--	--	--	--

Total Compensation Based on OECD PPP

	N	25th Percentile	Median	75th Percentile	Mean
24 Years or less	--	--	--	--	--
25 - 34 Years	13	$16,608	$31,142	$68,246	$53,326
35 - 44 Years	18	$37,000	$66,258	$97,000	$70,506
45 - 54 Years	16	$56,750	$71,913	$114,000	$122,263
55 - 64 Years	--	--	--	--	--
65+ Years	--	--	--	--	--

Middle East

Total Compensation Based on Exchange Rate

	N	25th Percentile	Median	75th Percentile	Mean
24 Years or less	--	--	--	--	--
25 - 34 Years	--	--	--	--	--
35 - 44 Years	15	$37,917	$60,000	$96,444	$66,782
45 - 54 Years	--	--	--	--	--
55 - 64 Years	--	--	--	--	--
65+ Years	--	--	--	--	--

Total Compensation Based on OECD PPP

	N	25th Percentile	Median	75th Percentile	Mean
24 Years or less	--	--	--	--	--
25 - 34 Years	--	--	--	--	--
35 - 44 Years	13	$40,850	$66,000	$98,222	$72,502
45 - 54 Years	--	--	--	--	--
55 - 64 Years	--	--	--	--	--
65+ Years	--	--	--	--	--

Compensation by Education

On a global basis, there was a predictable relationship between mean total compensation and formal education. Respondents with only high school degrees had a mean total compensation of $71,538, while respondents with doctoral degrees had a mean total compensation of $93,610 (see page 138).

The relationship between mean total compensation and formal education was even more pronounced within the United States (see page 139). Respondents with only high school degrees had a mean total compensation of $78,508, compared to respondents with doctoral degrees who earned $109,639 in mean total compensation.

The relationship between mean total compensation and formal education was less dramatic in Canada because the relationship was impacted by insufficient data at the highest and lowest educational levels. Canadian respondents with some college earned $55,685 in mean total compensation, while their counterparts with master's degrees averaged $65,190 in total compensation. Figures for Europe (see page 143) did not reflect the expected relationship between formal education and mean total compensation. Respondents with master's and doctoral degrees had smaller mean total compensation than respondents with only undergraduate degrees (see pages 138 through 145).

Compensation by Education

Global

Total Compensation Based on Exchange Rate

	N	25th Percentile	Median	75th Percentile	Mean
High school degree or equivalent	26	$44,851	$61,917	$95,850	$71,538
Some college/AA degree or equivalent	113	$51,068	$70,000	$90,000	$78,151
College degree or equivalent	541	$52,205	$72,000	$91,085	$76,549
Master's degree or equivalent	452	$60,558	$79,000	$100,000	$90,533
Doctoral degree or equivalent	47	$64,000	$92,000	$105,000	$93,610

Total Compensation Based on OECD PPP

	N	25th Percentile	Median	75th Percentile	Mean
High school degree or equivalent	26	$52,868	$67,125	$100,050	$78,379
Some college/AA degree or equivalent	113	$55,550	$70,000	$90,000	$79,775
College degree or equivalent	539	$57,265	$74,800	$93,000	$79,210
Master's degree or equivalent	449	$63,763	$80,000	$100,000	$93,111
Doctoral degree or equivalent	47	$69,000	$92,000	$105,000	$93,434

Compensation by Education

United States

Total Compensation Based on Exchange Rate

	N	25th Percentile	Median	75th Percentile	Mean
High school degree or equivalent	12	$56,000	$71,000	$106,650	$78,508
Some college/AA degree or equivalent	83	$57,000	$77,000	$96,500	$85,129
College degree or equivalent	313	$65,000	$80,000	$95,000	$83,649
Master's degree or equivalent	273	$70,100	$85,000	$102,000	$91,698
Doctoral degree or equivalent	26	$84,500	$95,000	$115,000	$109,639

Total Compensation Based on OECD PPP

	N	25th Percentile	Median	75th Percentile	Mean
High school degree or equivalent	12	$56,000	$71,000	$106,650	$78,508
Some college/AA degree or equivalent	83	$57,000	$77,000	$95,000	$84,589
College degree or equivalent	313	$65,000	$80,000	$95,000	$83,771
Master's degree or equivalent	273	$70,100	$85,000	$102,000	$91,698
Doctoral degree or equivalent	26	$84,500	$95,000	$115,000	$109,639

Compensation by Education

Canada

Total Compensation Based on Exchange Rate

	N	25th Percentile	Median	75th Percentile	Mean
High school degree or equivalent	--	--	--	--	--
Some college/AA degree or equivalent	17	$34,532	$52,205	$72,579	$55,685
College degree or equivalent	96	$44,011	$52,336	$63,367	$60,635
Master's degree or equivalent	44	$38,290	$52,907	$63,598	$65,190
Doctoral degree or equivalent	--	--	--	--	--

Total Compensation Based on OECD PPP

	N	25th Percentile	Median	75th Percentile	Mean
High school degree or equivalent	--	--	--	--	--
Some college/AA degree or equivalent	17	$43,589	$65,898	$77,666	$64,885
College degree or equivalent	96	$51,282	$63,587	$74,910	$67,918
Master's degree or equivalent	44	$46,616	$63,196	$76,935	$76,303
Doctoral degree or equivalent	--	--	--	--	--

Compensation by Education

Asia

Total Compensation Based on Exchange Rate

	N	25th Percentile	Median	75th Percentile	Mean
High school degree or equivalent	--	--	--	--	--
Some college/AA degree or equivalent	--	--	--	--	--
College degree or equivalent	41	$46,750	$81,313	$118,119	$89,332
Master's degree or equivalent	38	$73,306	$100,000	$116,700	$136,927
Doctoral degree or equivalent	--	--	--	--	--

Total Compensation Based on OECD PPP

	N	25th Percentile	Median	75th Percentile	Mean
High school degree or equivalent	--	--	--	--	--
Some college/AA degree or equivalent	--	--	--	--	--
College degree or equivalent	41	$49,121	$76,112	$107,795	$87,691
Master's degree or equivalent	38	$63,659	$82,500	$106,823	$129,417
Doctoral degree or equivalent	--	--	--	--	--

Compensation by Education

Australia/New Zealand

Total Compensation Based on Exchange Rate

	N	25th Percentile	Median	75th Percentile	Mean
High school degree or equivalent	--	--	--	--	--
Some college/AA degree or equivalent	--	--	--	--	--
College degree or equivalent	38	$39,674	$50,000	$67,640	$54,994
Master's degree or equivalent	19	$40,000	$51,964	$80,000	$79,403
Doctoral degree or equivalent	--	--	--	--	--

Total Compensation Based on OECD PPP

	N	25th Percentile	Median	75th Percentile	Mean
High school degree or equivalent	--	--	--	--	--
Some college/AA degree or equivalent	--	--	--	--	--
College degree or equivalent	38	$49,905	$58,277	$88,197	$66,790
Master's degree or equivalent	19	$50,000	$74,234	$90,076	$100,968
Doctoral degree or equivalent	--	--	--	--	--

Compensation by Education

Europe

Total Compensation Based on Exchange Rate

	N	25th Percentile	Median	75th Percentile	Mean
High school degree or equivalent	--	--	--	--	--
Some college/AA degree or equivalent	--	--	--	--	--
College degree or equivalent	25	$51,069	$88,682	$109,888	$85,591
Master's degree or equivalent	31	$39,416	$60,000	$79,288	$70,864
Doctoral degree or equivalent	11	$40,000	$71,863	$94,800	$70,566

Total Compensation Based on OECD PPP

	N	25th Percentile	Median	75th Percentile	Mean
High school degree or equivalent	--	--	--	--	--
Some college/AA degree or equivalent	--	--	--	--	--
College degree or equivalent	25	$49,473	$90,361	$109,063	$85,901
Master's degree or equivalent	31	$38,195	$60,555	$86,000	$74,256
Doctoral degree or equivalent	11	$44,615	$70,793	$105,000	$73,160

Compensation by Education

Latin America

Total Compensation Based on Exchange Rate

	N	25th Percentile	Median	75th Percentile	Mean
High school degree or equivalent	--	--	--	--	--
Some college/AA degree or equivalent	--	--	--	--	--
College degree or equivalent	16	$36,000	$56,702	$74,825	$56,536
Master's degree or equivalent	27	$40,600	$70,000	$96,000	$99,314
Doctoral degree or equivalent	--	--	--	--	--

Total Compensation Based on OECD PPP

	N	25th Percentile	Median	75th Percentile	Mean
High school degree or equivalent	--	--	--	--	--
Some college/AA degree or equivalent	--	--	--	--	--
College degree or equivalent	16	$36,000	$67,172	$79,500	$62,105
Master's degree or equivalent	27	$48,000	$70,000	$96,000	$101,550
Doctoral degree or equivalent	--	--	--	--	--

Compensation by Education

Middle East

Total Compensation Based on Exchange Rate

	N	25th Percentile	Median	75th Percentile	Mean
High school degree or equivalent	--	--	--	--	--
Some college/AA degree or equivalent	--	--	--	--	--
College degree or equivalent	--	--	--	--	--
Master's degree or equivalent	15	$41,700	$65,000	$100,000	$73,917
Doctoral degree or equivalent	--	--	--	--	--

Total Compensation Based on OECD PPP

	N	25th Percentile	Median	75th Percentile	Mean
High school degree or equivalent	--	--	--	--	--
Some college/AA degree or equivalent	--	--	--	--	--
College degree or equivalent	--	--	--	--	--
Master's degree or equivalent	12	$43,775	$66,000	$124,750	$78,892
Doctoral degree or equivalent	--	--	--	--	--

Change in Compensation
Between 1998 and 1999

Respondents were asked to indicate the percentage change in their annual salary/earnings between 1998 and 1999. The median and mean percentage changes by geographic area are shown below.

Change in Annual Salary/Earnings
Between 1998 and 1999

	Mean % Change	Median % Change
Global	8.8%	5.0%
United States	8.8%	5.0%
Canada	7.0%	4.0%
Asia	6.6%	4.0%
Australia/New Zealand	10.2%	7.0%
Europe	9.0%	5.0%
Latin America	16.4%	10.0%
Middle East	7.4%	6.0%

Information below reflects the mean and median change in annual bonus/overtime between 1998 and 1999.

Change in Annual Bonus/Overtime
Between 1998 and 1999

	Mean % Change	Median % Change
Global	34.8%	5.0%
United States	42.1%	5.0%
Canada	30.5%	2.0%
Asia	9.9%	4.0%
Australia/New Zealand	37.4%	7.0%
Europe	26.6%	10.0%
Latin America	18.6%	11.0%
Middle East	12.0%	7.5%

Information below reflects the mean and median change in annual deferred compensation between 1998 and 1999.

Change in Annual Deferred Compensation
Between 1998 and 1999

	Mean % Change	Median % Change
Global	11.9%	0.0%
United States	13.0%	0.0%
Canada	11.9%	0.0%
Asia	5.4%	0.0%
Australia/New Zealand	2.0%	0.0%
Europe	11.9%	0.0%
Latin America	--	--
Middle East	--	--

Benefits

Benefits

On a global basis, three out of four respondents received insurance as part of their benefits package (see page 151). United States respondents (78%) and respondents from the Middle East (81%) were more likely to have insurance in their benefits packages.

Three out of four respondents' (76%) employers made retirement contributions to their retirement funds. The global figure was elevated by respondents in the United States, 85% of whom received retirement contributions from their employers.

Nearly half of respondents worldwide (47%) received performance incentives. There was little variation in this figure across countries and regions of the world.

Three out of ten respondents on a global basis received stock options. Respondents in the United States (36%) and Europe (34%) were more likely to receive stock options.

Respondents were less likely to receive other benefits that were listed in the study (see page 151). On a global basis, the following percentages of respondents received specific benefits:

> 20% - Relocation/travel bonus
> 18% - Club memberships
> 17% - Free participation in stock purchases
> 15% - Vehicle
> 14% - Tickets to events
> 13% - Holiday bonus
> 10% - Signing bonus
> 10% - Entertainment allowance
> 9% - At-risk bonus pay
> 9% - "Other" benefits
> 8% - Retention incentive
> 7% - Housing allowance
> 4% - Mortgage paid by employer

As the table on page 152 shows, full-time employed respondents were more likely than full-time, self-employed respondents to receive insurance, retirement contributions, and performance incentives. However, self-employed respondents were more likely to receive the following benefits:

> *Vehicle
> *Entertainment allowance
> *Club memberships
> *Tickets to events

Benefits

On a global basis, respondents were likely to receive the following benefits:

      58% - Laptop/home computers
      55% - Free parking
      42% - Cellular telephones

European respondents (70%) were more likely to receive laptop/home computers; Latin American (63%) and United States (62%) respondents were more likely to receive free parking; and respondents in Europe (69%) and Australia/New Zealand (69%) were more likely to receive cellular telephones.

Healthcare insurance was widely available to respondents worldwide with 92% having it. Respondents in the United States (97%) were more likely to have healthcare insurance.

Other insurance, which over three out of four respondents were offered, included the following:

      79% - Long-term disability
      77% - Dental insurance
      76% - Life insurance
      76% - Accidental death
      73% - Prescription drugs
      72% - Short-term disability

With minor exceptions, respondents in Canada and the United States were more likely than their counterparts in other parts of the world to have each of the benefits listed on page 153.

Over half of respondents (56%) received their benefits via a Standard Plan, while two in five (39%) had a Cafeteria Plan where they chose a certain number of benefits up to a given monetary value. Respondents in the United States were more likely to have Cafeteria Plans, while respondents from other regions of the world were more likely to have Standard Plans.

Benefits

Percent of respondents who received the following benefits

	Global	US	Canada	Asia	Australia /New Zealand	Middle East	Latin America	Europe
Insurance	73%	78%	76%	73%	28%	81%	62%	61%
Retirement contributions by employer	76%	85%	65%	48%	54%	73%	60%	71%
Performance incentive	47%	48%	49%	34%	54%	46%	51%	47%
Retention incentive	8%	8%	8%	9%	5%	12%	16%	5%
Signing bonus	10%	11%	5%	19%	2%	19%	13%	4%
Stock options	30%	36%	20%	18%	20%	15%	18%	34%
Relocation/travel bonus	20%	20%	18%	21%	11%	35%	20%	22%
Holiday bonus	13%	10%	13%	16%	17%	31%	27%	26%
Housing allowance/free housing	7%	5%	4%	31%	2%	46%	9%	5%
Free participation in stock purchases	17%	20%	23%	8%	5%	12%	9%	12%
Vehicle	15%	7%	14%	15%	40%	73%	31%	38%
Entertainment allowance	10%	9%	17%	11%	9%	12%	0%	9%
Club memberships	18%	17%	27%	14%	25%	15%	11%	19%
Tickets to cultural events, sporting events, etc.	14%	14%	22%	11%	6%	8%	0%	10%
At-risk bonus pay	9%	10%	7%	4%	14%	8%	7%	10%
Mortgage paid by employer until current house sold	4%	4%	7%	3%	0%	0%	2%	1%
Other benefits	9%	8%	10%	6%	14%	12%	13%	9%

Benefits

Global

Percent of respondents who received the following benefits

	Full-time employed	Full-time self-employed
Insurance	75%	39%
Retirement contributions by employer	77%	42%
Performance incentive	49%	22%
Retention incentive	9%	--
Signing bonus	10%	--
Stock options	31%	--
Relocation/travel bonus	20%	--
Holiday bonus	13%	--
Housing allowance/free housing	7%	--
Free participation in stock purchases	18%	--
Vehicle	14%	46%
Entertainment allowance	9%	25%
Club memberships	18%	27%
Tickets to cultural events, sporting events, etc.	14%	19%
At-risk bonus pay	9%	--
Mortgage paid by employer until current house sold	4%	--
Other benefits	9%	--

Benefits

Percent of respondents who receive the following benefits from their employer (or from their government)

	Global	US	Canada	Asia	Australia /New Zealand	Middle East	Latin America	Europe
Paid child care	5%	2%	6%	18%	1%	24%	9%	16%
Maternity (paternity) leave	38%	33%	55%	43%	36%	20%	28%	47%
Matched savings	18%	27%	5%	3%	0%	4%	9%	6%
Sabbatical with pay	4%	2%	4%	10%	3%	8%	13%	5%
Wellness program	20%	28%	15%	10%	3%	4%	4%	11%
Free parking	55%	62%	52%	18%	43%	52%	63%	49%
Adult dependent care	4%	4%	1%	4%	0%	12%	9%	4%
Cellular telephone	42%	34%	46%	41%	69%	56%	39%	69%
Laptop/home computer	58%	59%	58%	41%	57%	60%	48%	70%
Other	8%	7%	4%	13%	10%	32%	11%	7%

Percent of respondents who are offered the following types of insurance

	Global	US	Canada	Asia	Australia /New Zealand	Middle East	Latin America	Europe
Healthcare insurance	92%	97%	95%	86%	40%	84%	87%	87%
Long-term disability	79%	87%	89%	34%	42%	68%	45%	74%
Short-term disability	72%	80%	80%	33%	36%	52%	40%	65%
Accidental death	76%	78%	83%	55%	52%	92%	84%	64%
Vision insurance	55%	65%	67%	13%	14%	32%	24%	30%
Prescription drugs	73%	85%	88%	28%	20%	48%	24%	42%
Dental insurance	77%	91%	89%	34%	10%	44%	26%	44%
Life insurance	76%	89%	79%	24%	26%	48%	68%	42%
Professional liability	15%	10%	24%	9%	36%	32%	13%	28%
Other	3%	3%	2%	3%	8%	0%	3%	4%

Does your employer offer you a standard plan (a fixed set of benefits) or a cafeteria plan (you are allowed to choose a certain number of benefits up to a given monetary value)?

	Global	US	Canada	Asia	Australia /New Zealand	Middle East	Latin America	Europe
Standard plan	56%	46%	68%	85%	58%	64%	82%	78%
Cafeteria plan	39%	52%	27%	7%	13%	20%	8%	19%
Other	6%	3%	6%	9%	29%	24%	12%	3%

Reimbursement Levels for Professional Development

Respondents were reimbursed, on average, 91% of their academic tuition payments. This figure was slightly higher in Europe (94%), Canada (94%), Australia/New Zealand (93%), and the United States (92%).

Nearly all respondents worldwide received 98% of their expenses for professional seminars/workshops from their employers. This figure varied only slightly across regions of the world.

Nearly all (97%) respondents' professional association dues were reimbursed by employers. Reimbursement percentages were greater than 90% for each region of the world.

Reimbursement Levels for Professional Development

Reimbursement levels for academic tuition

	Global	US
N	774	517
Mean Reimbursement	91%	92%
Median Reimbursement	100%	100%
1% - 50% Reimbursement	10%	8%
51% - 99% Reimbursement	13%	15%
100% Reimbursement	77%	77%

Reimbursement levels for academic tuition

	Canada	Asia	Australia /New Zealand	Middle East	Latin America	Europe
N	138	29	38	--	19	21
Mean Reimbursement	94%	75%	93%	--	78%	94%
Median Reimbursement	100%	100%	100%	--	90%	100%
1 - 99% Reimbursement	15%	41%	21%	--	58%	14%
100% Reimbursement	86%	59%	79%	--	42%	86%

Reimbursement levels for professional seminars/workshops

	Global	US	Canada	Asia	Australia /New Zealand	Middle East	Latin America	Europe
N	949	582	158	51	53	18	30	20
Mean Reimbursement	98%	99%	98%	92%	100%	94%	98%	97%
Median Reimbursement	100%	100%	100%	100%	100%	100%	100%	100%
1 - 99% Reimbursement	4%	3%	3%	16%	--	17%	7%	4%
100% Reimbursement	96%	97%	97%	84%	100%	43%	93%	96%

Reimbursement levels for professional association dues

	Global	US	Canada	Asia	Australia /New Zealand	Middle East	Latin America	Europe
N	814	524	129	37	48	12	20	37
Mean Reimbursement	97%	98%	99%	93%	97%	100%	97%	91%
Median Reimbursement	100%	100%	100%	100%	100%	100%	100%	100%
1 - 99% Reimbursement	4%	4%	3%	11%	6%	--	5%	11%
100% Reimbursement	96%	96%	97%	89%	94%	100%	95%	89%

Retirement

Over eight out of ten respondents worldwide (84%) had a retirement plan. Respondents in the United States (98%) were most likely to receive a retirement plan. On a global basis, 401 (k) plans were the most common type of retirement plan with 46% of respondents having this option. The global figure was greatly affected by the 75% of United States respondents who had 401 (k) plans.

Defined benefit plans were the most popular plan in Asia and the Middle East, while defined contribution plans were more prevalent in Canada, Australia/New Zealand, and Europe.

Most respondents (79%) had a vesting period before their retirement plans were activated. Respondents in Asia (89%) and the United States (83%) were more likely to have vesting periods.

A plurality of respondents (32%) had a 3–5 years vesting period, while another one in five respondents (22%) had longer vesting periods. Vesting periods in the United States, Canada, and Europe were more likely to be less than 5 years, while respondents from the Middle East and Latin America were more likely to have longer vesting periods.

Retirement

If you or your employer has a retirement plan, what is it?

	Global	US	Canada	Asia	Australia /New Zealand	Middle East	Latin America	Europe
No retirement plan	16%	2%	27%	42%	40%	52%	44%	36%
Defined benefit	20%	20%	22%	32%	9%	20%	19%	12%
Defined contribution	15%	9%	28%	19%	31%	8%	19%	25%
IRA	3%	4%	1%	0%	0%	0%	0%	0%
Money purchase plan	1%	1%	2%	1%	1%	0%	2%	5%
401 (k)-type plan - employee only	9%	13%	2%	4%	1%	0%	0%	0%
401 (k)-type plan - employer match	46%	75%	8%	2%	0%	0%	0%	7%
Profit sharing	7%	9%	9%	0%	4%	4%	8%	1%
Simplified employee plan (SEP)	2%	2%	0%	2%	1%	8%	2%	1%
Supplementary executive plan	1%	1%	1%	0%	1%	0%	0%	5%
Tax sheltered annuity	1%	1%	2%	0%	1%	0%	0%	1%
Employee stock options	10%	15%	7%	1%	2%	4%	2%	3%
Flexible benefit plan	6%	8%	5%	2%	1%	0%	2%	7%
Other	5%	3%	9%	2%	13%	8%	4%	11%

Do you have a vesting period before you become eligible for retirement benefits?

	Global	US	Canada	Asia	Australia /New Zealand	Middle East	Latin America	Europe
No vesting period	21%	17%	26%	11%	45%	--	--	40%
Vesting period	79%	83%	74%	89%	55%	--	--	60%

Retirement

How long is the vesting period before you become eligible for retirement benefits?

	Global	US
N	1,001	686
No vesting period	21%	17%
6 Months	5%	6%
1 Year	11%	11%
2 Years	4%	2%
3 - 5 years	32%	41%
6+ Years	22%	19%
Other	5%	4%

How long is the vesting period before you become eligible for retirement benefits?

	Global	US	Canada	Asia	Australia /New Zealand	Middle East	Latin America	Europe
N	1,001	686	135	56	52	19	29	25
No vesting period	21%	17%	32%	14%	52%	26%	31%	46%
1 - 5 Years	52%	60%	48%	39%	17%	16%	21%	29%
6+ Years	22%	19%	17%	38%	17%	53%	38%	20%
Other	5%	4%	3%	9%	14%	5%	10%	5%

Paid Leave

On average, respondents received 19 vacation days annually. Respondents in the Middle East and Europe received significantly more vacation days.

On a global basis, respondents averaged 17 days of paid sick leave annually. Respondents in Latin America received significantly fewer paid sick leave days (8), while respondents in Europe received significantly more paid sick leave days (20).

Respondents worldwide received an average of 10 paid holidays. Respondents in Asia received considerably more holidays (18) than their counterparts in other regions of the world.

The concept of receiving paid personal days was common to much of the world, with the exception of Australia/ New Zealand and the Middle East. Respondents in the United States and Canada each received five days. Asian respondents received 13 paid personal days annually.

Paid Leave

Vacation days

	Global	US	Canada	Asia	Australia /New Zealand	Middle East	Latin America	Europe
N	**1,144**	**660**	**171**	**88**	**67**	**29**	**42**	**79**
1 - 5 Days	2%	1%	1%	12%	1%	3%	5%	1%
6 - 10 Days	14%	22%	4%	14%	0%	4%	5%	0%
11 - 15 Days	26%	31%	32%	22%	8%	10%	21%	0%
16 - 20 Days	28%	25%	36%	20%	79%	7%	14%	9%
21 - 30 Days	26%	19%	25%	22%	10%	55%	53%	79%
31+ Days	4%	2%	2%	10%	2%	21%	2%	11%
Number of Days in 1999								
Mean	19	18	19	20	20	27	22	27
Median	20	15	20	17	20	30	21	26

Sick days

	Global	US	Canada	Asia	Australia /New Zealand	Middle East	Latin America	Europe
N	**704**	**409**	**120**	**46**	**63**	**20**	**17**	**24**
1 - 5 Days	31%	34%	22%	37%	18%	30%	59%	37%
6 - 10 Days	31%	32%	29%	22%	52%	15%	--	21%
11 - 15 Days	18%	14%	29%	20%	8%	25%	29%	13%
16+ Days	11%	11%	9%	19%	11%	20%	6%	17%
Unlimited or varies	9%	9%	11%	2%	11%	10%	6%	12%
Number of Days in 1999								
Mean	17	17	16	12	19	13	8	20
Median	10	8	10	7	10	10	5	10

Holidays

	Global	US	Canada	Asia	Australia /New Zealand	Middle East	Latin America	Europe
N	**1,058**	**632**	**160**	**81**	**66**	**21**	**35**	**58**
1 - 5 Days	8%	8%	4%	4%	6%	14%	11%	12%
6 - 10 Days	64%	72%	56%	15%	62%	62%	66%	62%
11 - 15 Days	25%	19%	40%	48%	29%	14%	23%	23%
16+ Days	4%	1%	0%	33%	3%	10%	0%	3%
Number of Days in 1999								
Mean	10	9	10	18	10	10	9	10
Median	10	9	10	14	10	10	9	9

Paid Leave

Personal days entitled to in 1999

	Global	US	Canada	Asia	Australia /New Zealand	Middle East	Latin America	Europe
N	491	354	60	32	--	--	16	14
1 - 3 Days	52%	54%	57%	13%	--	--	50%	64%
4 - 7 Days	31%	31%	27%	31%	--	--	38%	21%
8 + Days	14%	13%	8%	53%	--	--	13%	14%
Unlimited or varies	3%	2%	8%	3%	--	--	--	--
Number of Days in 1999								
Mean	5	5	4	13	--	--	4	4
Median	3	3	3	8	--	--	4	3

Other days of paid leave entitled to in 1999

	Global	US	Canada	Asia	Australia /New Zealand	Middle East	Latin America	Europe
N	135	81	16	--	--	--	--	11
1 Day	24%	26%	6%	--	--	--	--	18%
2 - 3 Days	23%	23%	25%	--	--	--	--	36%
4 - 5 Days	14%	14%	19%	--	--	--	--	18%
6 - 10 Days	13%	11%	6%	--	--	--	--	18%
11 - 15 Days	4%	2%	13%	--	--	--	--	--
16 - 20 Days	4%	5%	--	--	--	--	--	--
21 - 30 Days	10%	9%	13%	--	--	--	--	--
31+ Days	4%	6%	--	--	--	--	--	9%
Varies	4%	4%	19%	--	--	--	--	--
Number of Days in 1999								
Mean	11	11	9	--	--	--	--	21
Median	4	3	5	--	--	--	--	3

Profile

PMP Certification

The number of employees who have earned the Project Management Professional (PMP) Certification increased as the number of employees engaged in project/program management at a given location increased (see pages 166 through 169). It was also true that the number of respondents with the PMP Certification increased as the number of employees engaged in project/program management in the entire organization increased. However, the number of employees who have earned the PMP Certification was not directly related to the number of employees at a site nor the number of employees within an entire organization.

Respondents on a global basis received the following three major types of support in their efforts for pursuing the PMP Certification:

*Examination fee was paid,
*Meetings/training experiences were paid, and
*Encouragement was offered by employers.

Individuals who had attained the PMP Certification also were likely to receive money from their employers to attend meetings to maintain the PMP Certification. Respondents' employers were also likely to encourage respondents who had earned the PMP Certification to maintain certification.

PMP Certification

Have you earned the PMP Certification?

	Global	US	Canada	Asia	Australia /New Zealand	Middle East	Latin America	Europe
N	1,231	705	181	99	75	77	50	30
Yes	36%	32%	34%	52%	53%	38%	40%	37%
No	64%	68%	66%	48%	47%	62%	60%	63%

Global

PMP Certification by number of employees engaged in project/program management at your location

	PMP	Non PMP
1 - 2 People	27%	73%
3 - 4 People	32%	68%
5 - 10 People	32%	68%
11 - 15 People	39%	61%
16 - 20 People	39%	61%
21 - 30 People	44%	56%
31+ People	44%	56%

United States

PMP Certification by number of employees engaged in project/program management at your location

	PMP	Non PMP
1 - 2 People	24%	76%
3 - 4 People	30%	70%
5 - 10 People	26%	74%
11 - 15 People	37%	63%
16 - 20 People	29%	71%
21 - 30 People	39%	61%
31+ People	42%	58%

PMP Certification

Global

PMP Certification by number of employees engaged in project/program management in the entire organization

	PMP	Non PMP
1 - 10 People	28%	72%
11 - 25 People	31%	69%
26 - 50 People	34%	66%
51 - 100 People	34%	66%
101 - 299 People	45%	55%
300+ People	48%	52%

United States

PMP Certification by number of employees engaged in project/program management in the entire organization

	PMP	Non PMP
1 - 10 People	22%	78%
11 - 25 People	26%	74%
26 - 50 People	33%	67%
51 - 100 People	33%	67%
101 - 299 People	40%	60%
300+ People	42%	58%

PMP Certification

Global

PMP Certification by number of employees at your location

	PMP	Non PMP
1 - 10 People	38%	62%
11 - 20 People	30%	70%
21 - 50 People	39%	61%
51 - 100 People	32%	68%
101 - 200 People	34%	66%
201 - 500 People	37%	63%
501 - 1000 People	43%	57%
1001+ People	37%	63%

United States

PMP Certification by number of employees at your location

	PMP	Non PMP
1 - 10 People	31%	69%
11 - 20 People	31%	69%
21 - 50 People	37%	63%
51 - 100 People	28%	72%
101 - 200 People	28%	72%
201 - 500 People	31%	69%
501 - 1000 People	38%	62%
1001+ People	33%	67%

PMP Certification

Global

PMP Certification by employees in the entire organization

	PMP	Non PMP
1 - 50 People	37%	63%
51 - 100 People	35%	65%
101 - 200 People	37%	64%
201 - 500 People	35%	65%
501 - 1,000 People	25%	75%
1,001 - 5,000 People	39%	61%
5,001 - 10,000 People	31%	69%
10,001 - 20,000 People	31%	69%
20,001+ People	39%	61%

United States

PMP Certification by employees in the entire organization

	PMP	Non PMP
1 - 50 People	31%	69%
51 - 100 People	38%	62%
101 - 200 People	33%	67%
201 - 500 People	31%	69%
501 - 1,000 People	21%	79%
1,001 - 5,000 People	31%	69%
5,001 - 10,000 People	30%	70%
10,001 - 20,000 People	23%	77%
20,001+ People	35%	65%

Number of Individuals Who Have Earned PMP Certification at Office/Site

Global

Number of individuals who have earned PMP Certification at office/site

	N	%
0 People	433	40%
1 Person	206	19%
2 People	119	11%
3 People	76	7%
4 - 10 People	159	14%
11+ People	101	9%
Median = 1 Person		

United States

Number of individuals who have earned PMP Certification at office/site

	N	%
0 People	260	41%
1 Person	122	20%
2 People	65	10%
3 People	40	6%
4 - 10 People	94	15%
11+ People	51	8%
Median = 1 Person		

Canada

Number of individuals who have earned PMP Certification at office/site

	N	%
0 People	75	46%
1 - 3 People	61	38%
4+ People	26	16%
Median = 1 Person		

Asia

Number of individuals who have earned PMP Certification at office/site

	N	%
0 People	20	22%
1 - 3 People	29	33%
4+ People	40	45%
Median = 3 People		

Number of Individuals Who Have Earned PMP Certification at Office/Site

Australia/New Zealand

Number of individuals who have earned PMP Certification at office/site

	N	%
0 People	19	29%
1 - 3 People	26	39%
4+ People	21	32%
Median = 2 People		

Europe

Number of individuals who have earned PMP Certification at office/site

	N	%
0 People	25	40%
1 - 3 People	17	28%
4+ People	20	32%
Median = 1 Person		

Latin America

Number of individuals who have earned PMP Certification at office/site

	N	%
0 People	16	33%
1 - 3 People	25	52%
4+ People	--	--
Median = 1 Person		

Middle East

Number of individuals who have earned PMP Certification at office/site

	N	%
0 People	14	58%
1 - 3 People	10	42%
4+ People	--	--
Median = 0 People		

Support for PMP Certification at Office/Site

Percent of respondents who receive support for striving for PMP Certification at office/site

	Global	US	Canada	Asia	Australia /New Zealand	Middle East	Latin America	Europe
Paid leave	18%	16%	16%	18%	24%	20%	24%	31%
Pay for meetings/training	65%	71%	75%	36%	43%	36%	45%	66%
Pay for examination application fee	68%	69%	74%	56%	70%	40%	60%	69%
Recommends striving for PMP Certification	57%	57%	60%	41%	22%	52%	56%	57%
Requires PMP Certification	11%	10%	8%	14%	16%	8%	20%	17%
Rewards PMP Certification	17%	19%	14%	12%	16%	16%	18%	17%
Other	4%	4%	3%	4%	1%	1%	1%	1%

Percent of respondents who receive support for maintaining PMP Certification at office/site

	Global	US	Canada	Asia	Australia /New Zealand	Middle East	Latin America	Europe
Paid leave	15%	13%	13%	19%	14%	22%	22%	23%
Pay for meetings/training	61%	66%	74%	34%	41%	35%	47%	59%
Recommends maintaining PMP Certification	58%	56%	69%	51%	62%	65%	69%	50%
Requires maintaining PMP Certification	10%	8%	9%	15%	14%	4%	11%	16%
Rewards maintaining PMP Certification	10%	11%	9%	4%	5%	13%	16%	11%
Other	2%	2%	1%	0%	1%	1%	0%	1%

Employment Status

An overwhelming majority of respondents were full-time employed. This was true throughout the world.

Global

Category that reflects your employment status

	N	%
Full-time employed	1,182	92%
Full-time self-employed	72	7%
Student	--	--
Part-time employed	--	--
Part-time self-employed	--	--
Retired	--	--
Currently unemployed	--	--

United States

Category that reflects your employment status

	N	%
Full-time employed	698	95%
Full-time self-employed	25	3%
Student	--	--
Part-time employed	--	--
Part-time self-employed	--	--
Retired	--	--
Currently unemployed	--	--

Canada

Category that reflects your employment status

	N	%
Full-time employed	186	98%
Student	--	--
Part-time employed	--	--

Employment Status

Asia

Category that reflects your employment status

	N	%
Full-time employed	99	99%
Part-time employed	--	--

Australia/New Zealand

Category that reflects your employment status

	N	%
Full-time employed	97	98%
Part-time employed	--	--

Europe

Category that reflects your employment status

	N	%
Full-time employed	98	98%
Part-time employed	--	--

Latin America

Category that reflects your employment status

	N	%
Full-time employed	49	96%
Part-time employed	--	--

Middle East

Category that reflects your employment status

	N	%
Full-time employed	28	97%
Part-time employed	--	--

Number of Hours Worked
in a Typical Week

Three out of four respondents (75%) worked more than 40 hours per week. Respondents in the United States, the Middle East, and Europe were more likely to work more than 40 hours per week.

Number of hours worked in a typical week

	Global	US
1 - 40 Hours	25%	19%
41 - 45 Hours	25%	27%
46 - 50 Hours	31%	35%
51 - 55 Hours	7%	8%
56 - 60 Hours	9%	9%
61 + Hours	3%	2%

Number of hours worked in a typical week

	Canada	Asia	Australia /New Zealand	Middle East	Latin America	Europe
1 - 40 Hours	42%	44%	21%	18%	30%	19%
41+ Hours	58%	56%	79%	82%	70%	81%

Title/Position That Best Fits You within Your Organization

The most common title, by far, for respondents in the study was Project Manager. In fact, more than 50% of respondents in the study were Project or Program Managers with another 18% in higher level positions.

Global
The title/position that best fits you within your organization

	N	%
CEO, CFO, CIO, etc.	43	3%
Senior Management	92	7%
Director of Project/Program Management	105	8%
Professor/Academic	10	1%
Program Manager	159	12%
Project Manager	506	40%
Project Management Consultant/Advisor	94	7%
Project Engineer	31	2%
Project Team Leader	61	5%
Project Coordinator	33	3%
Project Planner/Scheduler	22	2%
Project Administrator	10	1%
Project Team Member	17	1%
Researcher	10	1%
Trainer	--	--
Other	80	6%

Title/Position That Best Fits You within Your Organization

United States

The title/position that best fits you within your organization

	N	%
CEO, CFO, CIO, etc.	13	2%
Senior Management	42	6%
Director of Project/Program Management	58	8%
Professor/Academic	--	--
Program Manager	112	15%
Project Manager	130	42%
Project Management Consultant/Advisor	46	6%
Project Engineer	13	2%
Project Team Leader	35	5%
Project Coordinator	18	2%
Project Planner/Scheduler	13	2%
Project Administrator	--	--
Project Team Member	--	--
Researcher	--	--
Trainer	--	--
Other	52	7%

Canada

The title/position that best fits you within your organization

	N	%
Upper Management	39	20%
Management	115	61%
Project Member	23	12%
Other	12	6%

Asia

The title/position that best fits you within your organization

	N	%
Upper Management	22	22%
Management	55	55%
Project Member	12	12%
Other	11	11%

Title/Position That Best Fits You within Your Organization

Australia/New Zealand

The title/position that best fits you within your organization

	N	%
Upper Management	14	18%
Management	55	71%
Project Member	--	--
Other	--	--

Europe

The title/position that best fits you within your organization

	N	%
Upper Management	22	27%
Management	47	57%
Project Member	--	--
Other	--	--

Latin America

The title/position that best fits you within your organization

	N	%
Upper Management	16	33%
Management	22	44%
Project Member	--	--
Other	--	--

Middle East

The title/position that best fits you within your organization

	N	%
Upper Management	12	43%
Management	--	--
Project Member	--	--
Other	--	--

Your Organization's Industry Affiliation

Respondents to the study were allowed to check one or more industry affiliations for their organizations. Most common industry affiliations were as follows:

28% - Information Technology,
20% - Consulting,
19% - Computers/Software/DP,
17% - Telecommunications,
16% - Engineering,
13% - E-business,
11% - Commercial/Heavy Industrial Construction, and
10% - Web Technology.

Your Organization's Industry Affiliation

Global

Describe your organization's industry affiliation that best reflects the industry focus of your organization

	N	%
Construction		
Commercial/Heavy Industrial	140	11%
Residential	34	3%
Other Construction	39	3%
Other Business Activities		
Academia	27	2%
Aerospace	38	3%
Architecture/Design	52	4%
Arts/Entertainment/Broadcasting	--	--
Automation Services	41	3%
Business Management	129	10%
City Management	--	--
Computers/Software/DP	241	19%
Consulting	257	20%
Defense	53	4%
E-Business	163	13%
Economics/Finance	21	2%
Education/Training	59	5%
Environmental/Waste/Sewage	53	4%
Engineering	198	16%
Financial Services	111	9%
Health/Human/Social Services	45	4%
Information Technology	362	28%
International Development	26	2%
Legal	11	1%
Printing/Publishing	10	1%
Public Administration/ Government	66	5%
Real Estate/Insurance	20	2%
Recreation	--	--
Supply Chain	42	3%
Systems Security	29	2%
Telecommunications	215	17%
Transportation	54	4%
Urban Development	15	1%
Utilities	71	6%

Your Organization's Industry Affiliation

Global

Describe your organization's industry affiliation that best reflects the industry focus of your organization

	N	%
Other Business Activities (cont.)		
Web Technology	126	10%
Other Business Activities	87	7%
Resources		
Agriculture	--	--
Coal/Gas/Oil	40	3%
Ferrous Mining	--	--
Forestry	--	--
Non-ferrous Mining	--	--
Manufacturing		
Automotive	41	3%
Chemical	24	2%
Concrete/Clay/Glass/ Stone	--	--
Electrical/Electronic	64	5%
Food	13	1%
Machinery/Metals	19	2%
Paper	--	--
Petroleum	26	2%
Pharmaceutical	40	3%
Plastics	--	--
Textiles/Fabrics	--	--
Wood	--	--
Other Manufacturing	29	2%

Your Role within the Organization

Over three out of five respondents described their role within their organizations as project/program management. Other frequently mentioned roles included the following:

16% - Consulting,
16% - Information/Computers, and
15% - Time Management/Scheduling/Planning.

Your Role within the Organization

Describe your role within your organization

	N	%
Engineering		
Chemical	--	--
Civil	54	4%
Electrical	29	2%
Electronics	15	1%
Environment	16	1%
Industrial	19	1%
Mechanical	40	3%
Other Engineering	34	3%
Management		
Communications	79	6%
Configuration	40	3%
Contract/Procurement	110	9%
Corporate/Administrative	92	8%
Cost	111	9%
Critical Chain	30	2%
Earned Value	60	5%
Human Resources	53	4%
Information/Computer	194	16%
Materials	23	2%
Project/Program	747	61%
Quality	104	8%
Records	23	2%
Risk/Safety	65	5%
Scope/Technical	112	9%
Site/Facility	35	3%
Time Management/Scheduling/Planning	189	15%
Other		
Consulting	197	16%
Distribution	--	--
Finance	13	1%
Financial Services	--	--
Legal	--	--
Marketing/Business Development/Sales	65	5%
Production	13	1%
Project Accounting/Audit	40	3%
Public Relations	--	--
Research/Product Development	41	3%
Service & Outsourcing	42	3%
Teaching/Training	63	5%
Web Strategist/Technologist	11	1%
Other	21	2%

Scope of Your Responsibilities

On a global basis, nearly half of respondents (45%) reported that Level 3 best fit their scope of responsibilities. Level 3 was described as follows:

> Responsible for directing large projects or a multitude of smaller projects. Manage all aspects of project, from beginning to end, with direct accountability for project execution while leading a team, or teams, to accomplish specific objectives in a given time frame and with limited resources.

Results for the United States were similar to global results with Level 3 being the most prominent by far.

Scope of Your Responsibilities

Global
Identify the scope of your responsibilities

	N	%
Level 1	128	10%
Level 2	160	13%
Level 3	565	45%
Level 4	150	12%
Level 5	97	8%
Level 6	28	2%
Level 7	17	1%
Level 8	28	2%
Level 9	22	2%
Level 10	32	3%
Level 11	32	2%

United States
Identify the scope of your responsibilities

	N	%
Level 1	128	8%
Level 2	160	14%
Level 3	565	47%
Level 4	150	12%
Level 5	97	7%
Level 6	28	2%
Level 7	17	2%
Level 8	28	2%
Level 9	22	1%
Level 10	32	3%
Level 11	32	2%

Canada
Identify the scope of your responsibilities

	N	%
Levels 1 - 2	40	22%
Level 3	84	46%
Levels 4 - 10	53	29%
Level 11	--	--

Scope of Your Responsibilities

Asia

Identify the scope of your responsibilities

	N	%
Levels 1 - 2	22	23%
Level 3	37	39%
Levels 4 - 10	36	38%
Level 11	--	--

Australia/New Zealand

Identify the scope of your responsibilities

	N	%
Levels 1 - 2	22	29%
Level 3	32	42%
Levels 4 - 10	22	29%
Level 11	--	--

Europe

Identify the scope of your responsibilities

	N	%
Levels 1 - 2	17	21%
Level 3	33	40%
Levels 4 - 10	28	34%
Level 11	--	--

Latin America

Identify the scope of your responsibilities

	N	%
Levels 1 - 2	17	35%
Level 3	20	42%
Levels 4 - 10	--	--
Level 11	--	--

Middle East

Identify the scope of your responsibilities

	N	%
Levels 1 - 2	11	37%
Level 3	--	--
Levels 4 - 10	12	40%
Level 11	--	--

Geographic Scope of the Projects in Which You Are Currently Engaged In/Managed

Slightly more than one third of respondents (37%) described the geographic scope of their projects as local. Projects with Multi-State/Province or Within One Country's borders were also frequently mentioned.

Geographic Scope of the Projects in Which You Are Currently Engaged In/Managed

Global

The geographic scope of the projects in which you are currently engaged in/managed

	N	%
Local	453	37%
State/Province	280	23%
Multi-State/Province	391	32%
Within One Country	397	32%
Multiple Countries	299	24%
Multiple Continents	208	17%

United States

The geographic scope of the projects in which you are currently engaged in/managed

	N	%
Local	276	38%
State/Province	156	22%
Multi-State/Province	279	39%
Within One Country	188	26%
Multiple Countries	151	21%
Multiple Continents	128	18%

Canada

The geographic scope of the projects in which you are currently engaged in/managed

	N	%
Within One Country	148	82%
Multiple Countries /Multiple Continents	58	32%

Asia

The geographic scope of the projects in which you are currently engaged in/managed

	N	%
Within One Country	65	87%
Multiple Countries /Multiple Continents	40	41%

Geographic Scope of the Projects in Which You Are Currently Engaged In/Managed

Australia/New Zealand

The geographic scope of the projects in which you are currently engaged in/managed

	N	%
Within One Country	66	87%
Multiple Countries /Multiple Continents	22	29%

Europe

The geographic scope of the projects in which you are currently engaged in/managed

	N	%
Within One Country	48	59%
Multiple Countries /Multiple Continents	45	55%

Latin America

The geographic scope of the projects in which you are currently engaged in/managed

	N	%
Within One Country	41	87%
Multiple Countries /Multiple Continents	--	--

Middle East

The geographic scope of the projects in which you are currently engaged in/managed

	N	%
Within One Country	21	79%
Multiple Countries /Multiple Continents	--	--

Mean Budget Size of the Typical Project in Which You Are Now Engaged In/Managed

Budget size of projects on which respondents worked varied widely with 10% of respondents working on projects whose budgets averaged less than $100,000, and 26% of respondents working on projects with mean budgets greater than $10 million. The estimated median budget size of project was $2 million, while the estimated mean budget size was $55 million. The vast difference between the estimated median and estimated mean budget sizes is due to the relatively few very large projects on which some respondents worked. Below are estimated median budget sizes for projects on which respondents worked for different parts of the world.

Geographic Area	Estimated Median Project Size
Global	$2.0 Million
United States	$1.7 Million
Canada	$0.8 Million
Asia	$23.0 Million
Australia/New Zealand	$1.3 Million
Europe	$1.9 Million
Latin America	$12.0 Million
Middle East	$22.0 Million

Mean Budget Size of the Typical Project in Which You Are Now Engaged In/Managed

Global

Mean budget size of the typical project in
which you are now engaged in/managed

	N	%
<$100,000	128	10%
$100,000 - $249,000	131	10%
$250,000 - $499,999	124	10%
$500,000 - $999,999	125	10%
$1.0 Million - $1.99 Million	128	10%
$2.0 Million - $2.99 Million	92	7%
$3.0 Million - $3.99 Million	58	5%
$4.0 Million - $4.99 Million	36	3%
$5.0 Million - $9.99 Million	113	9%
$10.0 Million - $24.99 Million	101	8%
$25.0 Million - $49.99 Million	57	5%
$50.0 Million - $99.99 Million	55	4%
$100.0 Million - $499.99 Million	73	6%
$500.0 Million - $999.99 Million	20	2%
$1.0 Billion - $9.99 Billion	11	1%
≥$10.0 Billion	--	--

United States

Mean budget size of the typical project in
which you are now engaged in/managed

	N	%
<$100,000	76	11%
$100,000 - $249,000	72	10%
$250,000 - $499,999	69	10%
$500,000 - $999,999	77	11%
$1.0 Million - $1.99 Million	86	12%
$2.0 Million - $2.99 Million	56	8%
$3.0 Million - $3.99 Million	35	5%
$4.0 Million - $4.99 Million	23	3%
$5.0 Million - $9.99 Million	67	9%
$10.0 Million - $24.99 Million	57	8%
$25.0 Million - $49.99 Million	24	3%
$50.0 Million - $99.99 Million	25	3%
$100.0 Million - $499.99 Million	36	5%
$500.0 Million - $999.99 Million	11	2%
$1.0 Billion - $9.99 Billion	--	--
≥$10.0 Billion	--	--

Mean Budget Size of the Typical Project in Which You Are Now Engaged In/Managed

Canada

Mean budget size of the typical project in
which you are now engaged in/managed

	N	%
<$500,000	72	44%
$500,000 - $1.99 Million	39	24%
$2.0 Million - $24.99 Million	35	22%
≥$25.0 Million	17	10%

Asia

Mean budget size of the typical project in
which you are now engaged in/managed

	N	%
<$500,000	12	13%
$500,000 - $1.99 Million	10	11%
$2.0 Million - $24.99 Million	25	27%
≥$25.0 Million	46	49%

Australia/New Zealand

Mean budget size of the typical project in
which you are now engaged in/managed

	N	%
<$500,000	29	41%
$500,000 - $1.99 Million	12	17%
$2.0 Million - $24.99 Million	24	34%
≥$25.0 Million	--	--

Mean Budget Size of the Typical Project in Which You Are Now Engaged In/Managed

Europe

Mean budget size of the typical project in which you are now engaged in/managed

	N	%
<$500,000	24	31%
$500,000 - $1.99 Million	14	18%
$2.0 Million - $24.99 Million	26	33%
≥$25.0 Million	14	18%

Latin America

Mean budget size of the typical project in which you are now engaged in/managed

	N	%
<$500,000	--	--
$500,000 - $1.99 Million	--	--
$2.0 Million - $24.99 Million	22	49%
≥$25.0 Million	11	24%

Middle East

Mean budget size of the typical project in which you are now engaged in/managed

	N	%
<$500,000	--	--
$500,000 - $1.99 Million	--	--
$2.0 Million - $24.99 Million	11	39%
≥$25.0 Million	15	54%

Current Number of Projects You Are Engaged In/Managed

The typical (defined by the median) respondent was engaged in/managed 3 projects. Of course, there was considerable variation across respondents in terms of how many projects they were engaged in/managed. For example, one in three respondents was engaged in/managed only 1 or 2 projects, while nearly three out of 10 respondents (28%) were engaged in/managed 6 or more projects. Figures for respondents working within the United States were similar to global figures. Estimated median number of projects engaged in/managed by respondents around the world are shown below.

Geographic Area	Estimated Median Number of Projects Engaged In/Managed
Global	3 Projects
United States	3 Projects
Canada	4 Projects
Asia	3 Projects
Australia/New Zealand	4 Projects
Europe	3 Projects
Latin America	4 Projects
Middle East	3 Projects

Current Number of Projects You Are Engaged In/Managed

Global

The current number of projects you are personally engaged in/managed

	N	%
1 Project	172	14%
2 Projects	210	18%
3 Projects	241	20%
4 Projects	132	11%
5 Projects	112	9%
6 - 10 Projects	183	15%
11+ Projects	151	13%

United States

The current number of projects you are personally engaged in/managed

	N	%
1 Project	95	14%
2 Projects	114	16%
3 Projects	135	20%
4 Projects	74	11%
5 Projects	61	9%
6 - 10 Projects	121	17%
11+ Projects	94	13%

Canada

The current number of projects you are personally engaged in/managed

	N	%
1 - 2 Projects	56	32%
3 - 7 Projects	78	44%
8+ Projects	43	24%

Asia

The current number of projects you are personally engaged in/managed

	N	%
1 - 2 Projects	34	37%
3 - 7 Projects	47	52%
8+ Projects	10	11%

Current Number of Projects You Are Engaged In/Managed

Australia/New Zealand

The current number of projects you are personally engaged in/managed

	N	%
1 - 2 Projects	27	36%
3 - 7 Projects	36	47%
8+ Projects	13	17%

Europe

The current number of projects you are personally engaged in/managed

	N	%
1 - 2 Projects	33	42%
3 - 7 Projects	36	46%
8+ Projects	10	12%

Latin America

The current number of projects you are personally engaged in/managed

	N	%
1 - 2 Projects	10	22%
3 - 7 Projects	31	69%
8+ Projects	--	--

Middle East

The current number of projects you are personally engaged in/managed

	N	%
1 - 2 Projects	11	41%
3 - 7 Projects	11	41%
8+ Projects	--	--

Approximate Number of People You Presently Supervise

The typical respondent worldwide supervised 10 people. One in six respondents (17%) supervised only 1 or 2 people, while one out of five respondents (19%) supervised more than 25 people. Estimated median numbers of people supervised by area of the world are shown below.

Geographic Area	Estimated Median Number of People Supervised
Global	10 People
United States	10 People
Canada	13 People
Asia	17 People
Australia/New Zealand	14 People
Europe	15 People
Latin America	23 People
Middle East	15 People

Approximate Number of People You Presently Supervise

Global

The approximate number of people you presently supervise

	N	%
1 - 2 People Supervised	70	7%
3 - 4 People Supervised	97	10%
5 - 6 People Supervised	114	12%
7 - 8 People Supervised	92	10%
9 - 10 People Supervised	102	11%
11 - 15 People Supervised	133	14%
16 - 20 People Supervised	95	10%
21 - 25 People Supervised	64	7%
26 - 50 People Supervised	97	10%
51+ People Supervised	77	9%

United States

The approximate number of people you presently supervise

	N	%
1 - 2 People Supervised	45	9%
3 - 4 People Supervised	58	11%
5 - 6 People Supervised	65	12%
7 - 8 People Supervised	51	10%
9 - 10 People Supervised	49	10%
11 - 15 People Supervised	75	15%
16 - 20 People Supervised	41	8%
21 - 25 People Supervised	41	8%
26 - 50 People Supervised	51	10%
51+ People Supervised	42	7%

Canada

The approximate number of people you presently supervise

	N	%
1 - 5 People Supervised	36	26%
6 - 24 People Supervised	84	60%
25+ People Supervised	20	14%

Asia

The approximate number of people you presently supervise

	N	%
1 - 5 People Supervised	14	18%
6 - 24 People Supervised	42	53%
25+ People Supervised	23	29%

Approximate Number of People You Presently Supervise

Australia/New Zealand

The approximate number of people you presently supervise

	N	%
1 - 5 People Supervised	16	27%
6 - 24 People Supervised	36	61%
25+ People Supervised	--	--

Europe

The approximate number of people you presently supervise

	N	%
1 - 5 People Supervised	15	23%
6 - 24 People Supervised	35	52%
25+ People Supervised	17	25%

Latin America

The approximate number of people you presently supervise

	N	%
1 - 5 People Supervised	--	--
6 - 24 People Supervised	23	52%
25+ People Supervised	21	48%

Middle East

The approximate number of people you presently supervise

	N	%
1 - 5 People Supervised	--	--
6 - 24 People Supervised	11	44%
25+ People Supervised	--	--

Number of Employees in Project/ Program Management at Your Location

The typical respondent had 11 people at his location who were involved in project/program management. One in five respondents (21%) had only 1 or 2 people at his location who were involved in project/program management, while one in four respondents (23%) worked with at least 30 others in project/program management. Estimated median number of employees involved in project/program management at respondents' locations are shown below.

Geographic Area	Estimated Median Number of Employees in Project/Program Management at Location
Global	11 People
United States	10 People
Canada	9 People
Asia	9 People
Australia/New Zealand	9 People
Europe	25 People
Latin America	23 People
Middle East	16 People

Number of Employees in Project/ Program Management at Your Location

Global

Total number of employees engaged in project/program management at your office or location or division

	N	%
1 - 2 People	109	9%
3 - 4 People	137	12%
5 - 10 People	328	28%
11 - 15 People	113	10%
16 - 20 People	101	8%
21 - 30 People	116	10%
31+ People	268	23%

United States

Total number of employees engaged in project/program management at your office or location or division

	N	%
1 - 2 People	63	9%
3 - 4 People	85	13%
5 - 10 People	202	30%
11 - 15 People	74	11%
16 - 20 People	50	7%
21 - 30 People	56	8%
31+ People	149	22%

Canada

Total number of employees engaged in project/program management at your office or location or division

	N	%
1 - 10 People	93	53%
11 - 50 People	65	37%
51+ People	17	10%

Asia

Total number of employees engaged in project/program management at your office or location or division

	N	%
1 - 10 People	93	53
11 - 50 People	65	37
51+ People	17	10

Number of Employees in Project/ Program Management at Your Location

Australia/New Zealand

Total number of employees engaged in project/program management at your office or location or division

	N	%
1 - 10 People	37	52%
11 - 50 People	24	34%
51+ People	10	14%

Europe

Total number of employees engaged in project/program management at your office or location or division

	N	%
1 - 10 People	25	33%
11 - 50 People	36	47%
51+ People	15	20%

Latin America

Total number of employees engaged in project/program management at your office or location or division

	N	%
1 - 10 People	18	39%
11 - 50 People	16	35%
51+ People	12	26%

Middle East

Total number of employees engaged in project/program management at your office or location or division

	N	%
1 - 10 People	12	44%
11 - 50 People	12	44%
51+ People	--	--

Number of Employees in Project/ Program Management in Your Organization

The typical respondent had 48 people in his organization who were involved in project/program management. One in five respondents (22%) had 10 or fewer people in his organization who were involved in project/ program management, while the same percentage of respondents had at least 300 others in project/program management throughout their organization. Estimated median number of employees involved in project/program management in respondents' organizations are shown below.

Geographic Area	Estimated Median Number of Employees in Project/Program Management at Location
Global	48 People
United States	47 People
Canada	133 People
Asia	160 People
Australia/New Zealand	141 People
Europe	182 People
Latin America	155 People
Middle East	146 People

Number of Employees in Project/ Program Management in Your Organization

Global

Total number of employees engaged in project/program management in the entire organization

	N	%
1 - 10 People	205	22%
11 - 25 People	135	14%
26 - 50 People	157	16%
51 - 100 People	139	14%
101 - 300 People	119	12%
301+ People	208	22%

United States

Total number of employees engaged in project/program management in the entire organization

	N	%
1 - 10 People	115	21%
11 - 25 People	85	16%
26 - 50 People	84	15%
51 - 100 People	80	15%
101 - 300 People	69	13%
301+ People	111	20%

Canada

Total number of employees engaged in project/program management in the entire organization

	N	%
1 - 10 People	36	26%
11 - 300 People	80	57%
301+ People	25	17%

Asia

Total number of employees engaged in project/program management in the entire organization

	N	%
1 - 10 People	12	15%
11 - 300 People	43	53%
301+ People	26	32%

Number of Employees in Project/ Program Management in Your Organization

Australia/New Zealand

Total number of employees engaged in project/program management in the entire organization

	N	%
1 - 10 People	16	28%
11 - 300 People	28	48%
301+ People	14	24%

Europe

Total number of employees engaged in project/program management in the entire organization

	N	%
1 - 10 People	12	18%
11 - 300 People	36	54%
301+ People	19	28%

Latin America

Total number of employees engaged in project/program management in the entire organization

	N	%
1 - 10 People	--	--
11 - 300 People	27	73%
301+ People	--	--

Middle East

Total number of employees engaged in project/program management in the entire organization

	N	%
1 - 10 People	--	--
11 - 300 People	15	57%
301+ People	--	--

Number of Employees at Your Office or Location or Division

The typical respondent had 121 employees at his location. One in five respondents (18%) had 20 or fewer employees at his location, while 22% of respondents had at least 500 employees at his location. Estimated median number of employees at respondents' locations are shown below.

Geographic Area	Estimated Median Number of Employees at Location
Global	121 People
United States	140 People
Canada	310 People
Asia	330 People
Australia/New Zealand	455 People
Europe	345 People
Latin America	225 People
Middle East	335 People

Number of Employees at Your Office or Location or Division

Global

Total number of employees at your office or location or division

	N	%
1 - 10 People	131	11%
11 - 20 People	86	7%
21 - 50 People	179	15%
51 - 100 People	159	14%
101 - 200 People	179	15%
201 - 500 People	184	16%
501 - 1,000 People	95	8%
1,001+ People	163	14%

United States

Total number of employees at your office or location or division

	N	%
1 - 10 People	72	11%
11 - 20 People	48	7%
21 - 50 People	81	12%
51 - 100 People	99	14%
101 - 200 People	100	15%
201 - 500 People	114	17%
501 - 1,000 People	47	7%
1,000+ People	116	17%

Canada

Total number of employees at your office or location or division

	N	%
1 - 29 People	38	21%
30 - 600 People	106	59%
601+ People	35	20%

Asia

Total number of employees at your office or location or division

	N	%
1 - 29 People	17	19%
30 - 600 People	53	59%
601+ People	20	22%

Number of Employees at Your Office or Location or Division

Australia/New Zealand

Total number of employees at your office or location or division

	N	%
1 - 29 People	21	29%
30 - 600 People	42	57%
601+ People	10	14%

Europe

Total number of employees at your office or location or division

	N	%
1 - 29 People	13	18%
30 - 600 People	42	58%
601+ People	17	24%

Latin America

Total number of employees at your office or location or division

	N	%
1 - 29 People	15	32%
30 - 600 People	25	53%
601+ People	--	--

Middle East

Total number of employees at your office or location or division

	N	%
1 - 29 People	--	--
30 - 600 People	20	74%
601+ People	--	--

Number of Employees in the Entire Organization

The typical respondent had 2,050 employees in his organization. One in six respondents (17%) had 1,000 or fewer employees in his organization, while 24% of respondents had at least 10,000 employees in his organization. Estimated median number of employees in respondents' organizations are shown below.

Geographic Area	Estimated Median Number of Employees in Organization
Global	2,050 People
United States	2,990 People
Canada	760 People
Asia	755 People
Australia/New Zealand	605 People
Europe	910 People
Latin America	475 People
Middle East	790 People

Number of Employees in the Entire Organization

Global

Total number of employees in the entire organization

	N	%
1 - 50 People	125	11%
51 - 100 People	64	6%
101 - 200 People	65	6%
201 - 500 People	152	14%
501 - 1,000 People	76	7%
1,001 - 5,000 People	246	22%
5,001 - 10,000 People	108	10%
10,001 - 20,000 People	77	7%
20,001+ People	197	17%

United States

Total number of employees in the entire organization

	N	%
1 - 50 People	48	8%
51 - 100 People	39	6%
101 - 200 People	39	6%
201 - 500 People	85	13%
501 - 1,000 People	45	7%
1,001 - 5,000 People	134	21%
5,001 - 10,000 People	65	10%
10,001 - 20,000 People	47	8%
20,001+ People	135	21%

Canada

Total number of employees in the entire organization

	N	%
1 - 199 People	42	25%
200 - 1,499 People	100	58%
1,500+ People	30	17%

Asia

Total number of employees in the entire organization

	N	%
1 - 199 People	18	21%
200 - 1,499 People	57	68%
1,500+ People	--	--

Number of Employees in the Entire Organization

Australia/New Zealand

Total number of employees in the entire organization

	N	%
1 - 199 People	22	35%
200 - 1,499 People	31	48%
1,500+ People	11	17%

Europe

Total number of employees in the entire organization

	N	%
1 - 199 People	15	21%
200 - 1,499 People	39	53%
1,500+ People	19	26%

Latin America

Total number of employees in the entire organization

	N	%
1 - 199 People	15	37%
200 - 1,499 People	25	61%
1,500+ People	--	--

Middle East

Total number of employees in the entire organization

	N	%
1 - 199 People	--	--
200 - 1,499 People	22	79%
1,500+ People	--	--

Years Worked in Project Management

The typical respondent had worked in project management for 8 years. Three out of ten respondents (30%) had worked in project management for 5 or fewer years, while 21% of respondents had worked in project management for at least 15 years. Estimated median number of years respondents had worked in project management are shown below.

Geographic Area	Estimated Median Number of Years Worked in Project Management
Global	8 Years
United States	8 Years
Canada	7 Years
Asia	8 Years
Australia/New Zealand	10 Years
Europe	10 Years
Latin America	11 Years
Middle East	13 Years

Years Worked in Project Management

Global

Total number of years worked in project management

	N	%
1 - 2 Years	86	7%
3 - 5 Years	285	23%
6 - 10 Years	376	30%
11 - 15 Years	243	19%
16 - 20 Years	150	12%
21+ Years	115	9%

United States

Total number of years worked in project management

	N	%
1 - 2 Years	54	7%
3 - 5 Years	181	25%
6 - 10 Years	215	29%
11 - 15 Years	135	18%
16 - 20 Years	84	12%
21+ Years	63	9%

Canada

Total number of years worked in project management

	N	%
1 - 4 Years	41	23%
5 - 15 Years	102	57%
16+ Years	36	20%

Asia

Total number of years worked in project management

	N	%
1 - 4 Years	10	10%
5 - 15 Years	67	68%
16+ Years	21	22%

Years Worked in Project Management

Australia/New Zealand

Total number of years worked in project management

	N	%
1 - 4 Years	13	18%
5 - 15 Years	44	60%
16+ Years	17	23%

Europe

Total number of years worked in project management

	N	%
1 - 4 Years	14	18%
5 - 15 Years	47	59%
16+ Years	18	23%

Latin America

Total number of years worked in project management

	N	%
1 - 4 Years	--	--
5 - 15 Years	28	56%
16+ Years	14	28%

Middle East

Total number of years worked in project management

	N	%
1 - 4 Years	--	--
5 - 15 Years	14	48%
16+ Years	12	41%

Work Environment

Most respondents (84%) worked in a traditional office environment. The typical respondent was away from his office 5 days a month. On a global basis, 5% of respondents had a virtual office, and 86% of these individuals were at least somewhat satisfied with their virtual office arrangement. Of the 5% of respondents that answered "Other" for their work environment, most listed a combination of the work environments. Several respondents said that they worked at a client site.

Work Environment

Primary Work Environment

	Global	US	Canada	Asia	Australia /New Zealand	Middle East	Latin America	Europe
Traditional office	84%	83%	87%	94%	81%	90%	92%	74%
Virtual office	5%	6%	3%	4%	4%	0%	2%	11%
Office in home or residence	6%	7%	7%	2%	10%	0%	4%	6%
Other	5%	5%	3%	0%	5%	10%	2%	9%

In a typical month, how many days are you away from your primary work location?

	Global	US	Canada	Asia	Australia /New Zealand	Middle East	Latin America	Europe
N	988	555	146	86	59	23	43	69
1 - 3 Days	38%	42%	34%	29%	42%	30%	30%	23%
4 - 9 Days	36%	32%	45%	45%	31%	57%	30%	42%
10 - 30 Days	26%	26%	21%	26%	27%	13%	40%	35%
Number of Days Within a Month								
Mean	6	6	6	7	6	5	9	7
Median	5	4	5	5	5	4	7	5

Work Environment

Global
If you work primarily in a virtual office, how satisfied are you with this arrangement?

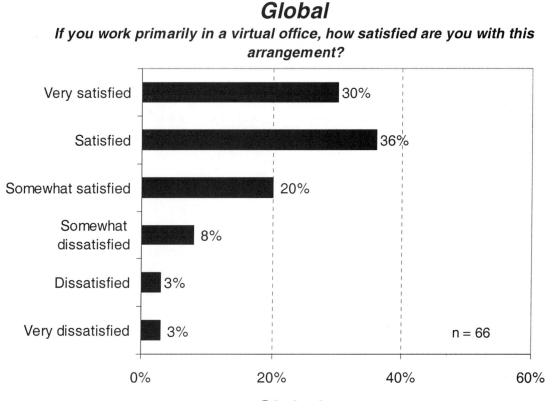

Very satisfied	30%
Satisfied	36%
Somewhat satisfied	20%
Somewhat dissatisfied	8%
Dissatisfied	3%
Very dissatisfied	3%

n = 66

Global
If you work primarily from an office in your home, for which of the following expenses do you receive financial support?

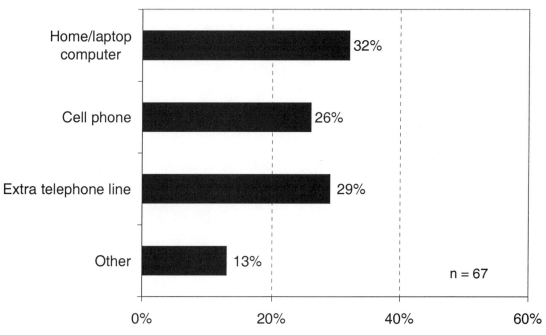

Home/laptop computer	32%
Cell phone	26%
Extra telephone line	29%
Other	13%

n = 67

Work History and Professional/ Personal Profile

The typical respondent had been with his current employer for 5 1/2 years, had changed employers at least once in the past 5 years. Three out of ten respondents (31%) had relocated with the same employer in the past 5 years.

Seven out of ten respondents (68%) had some type of career path; 45% had an informal or unstated career path, while 23% had a clearly defined, written career path. Nearly nine out of ten respondents (85%) claimed there was a career path connected to roles in upper management within their organizations for someone engaged in project management. Over seven out of ten respondents (72%) maintained there was a set of performance skills defined for those working in project or program management within their organizations.

Six out of ten respondents (58%) worked in the United States. Most of the United States respondents in the study worked in the Southeast (24%), the Midwest (24%), or the Northeast (22%). One in seven respondents responding to the study (15%) worked in Canada. Ontario and Quebec were the most heavily represented provinces.

The typical respondent to this study was 43 years old and had either a college (undergraduate) degree (46%) or a master's degree (39%). Three out of four respondents were male, and 63% had been a PMI member only a year or two.

Years Worked for Current Employer

Global

Total years worked for your current employer

	N	%
1 Year	210	17%
2 Years	154	12%
3 - 5 Years	264	21%
6 - 10 Years	191	15%
11 - 15 Years	140	11%
16 - 20 Years	122	10%
21+ Years	163	14%

United States

Total years worked for your current employer

	N	%
1 Year	145	20%
2 Years	87	12%
3 - 5 Years	161	22%
6 - 10 Years	100	14%
11 - 15 Years	83	11%
16 - 20 Years	69	9%
21+ Years	85	12%

Canada

Total years worked for your current employer

	N	%
1 - 2 Years	54	31%
3 - 5 Years	34	19%
6 - 10 Years	30	17%
11 - 15 Years	15	9%
16+ Years	43	24%

Asia

Total years worked for your current employer

	N	%
1 - 2 Years	11	11%
3 - 5 Years	18	18%
6 - 10 Years	12	12%
11 - 15 Years	12	12%
16+ Years	46	47%

Years Worked for Current Employer

Australia/New Zealand

Total years worked for your current employer

	N	%
1 - 2 Years	28	39%
3 - 5 Years	13	18%
6 - 10 Years	14	19%
11 - 15 Years	7	10%
16+ Years	10	14%

Europe

Total years worked for your current employer

	N	%
1 - 2 Years	21	27%
3 - 5 Years	17	22%
6 - 10 Years	20	27%
11 - 15 Years	--	--
16+ Years	13	17%

Latin America

Total years worked for your current employer

	N	%
1 - 2 Years	--	--
3 - 5 Years	10	21%
6 - 10 Years	--	--
11 - 15 Years	--	--
16+ Years	12	25%

Middle East

Total years worked for your current employer

	N	%
1 - 2 Years	--	--
3 - 5 Years	10	35
6 - 10 Years	--	--
11 - 15 Years	--	--
16+ Years	--	--

Changed Employers in the Past Five Years

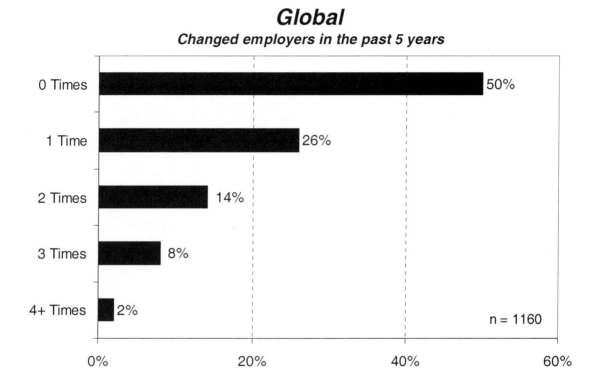

Global
Changed employers in the past 5 years

0 Times	50%
1 Time	26%
2 Times	14%
3 Times	8%
4+ Times	2%

n = 1160

0%   20%   40%   60%

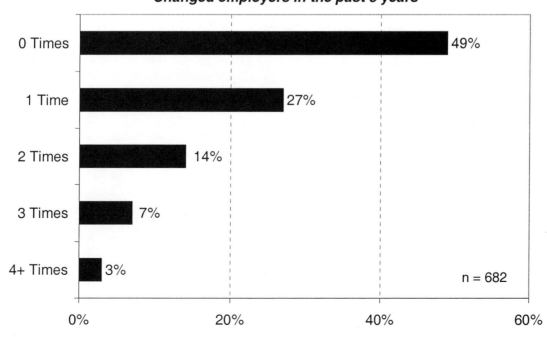

United States
Changed employers in the past 5 years

0 Times	49%
1 Time	27%
2 Times	14%
3 Times	7%
4+ Times	3%

n = 682

0%   20%   40%   60%

Changed Employers in the Past Five Years

Changed employers in the past 5 years

	Global	US	Canada	Asia	Australia /New Zealand	Middle East	Latin America	Europe
0 Times	50%	49%	49%	70%	44%	43%	57%	53%
1 Time	26%	27%	23%	14%	22%	33%	26%	22%
2+ Times	24%	24%	28%	16%	34%	24%	17%	25%

Relocated with the Same Employer in the Past Five Years

Global

Relocated with the same employer in the past 5 years

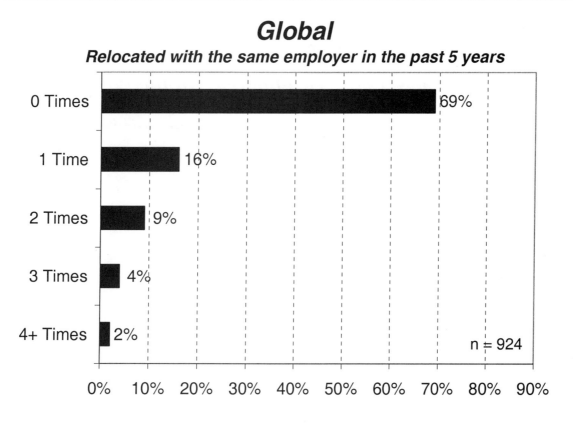

0 Times	69%
1 Time	16%
2 Times	9%
3 Times	4%
4+ Times	2%

n = 924

United States

Relocated with the same employer in the past 5 years

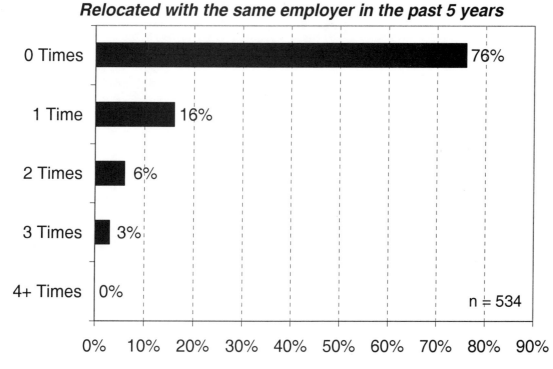

0 Times	76%
1 Time	16%
2 Times	6%
3 Times	3%
4+ Times	0%

n = 534

Relocated with the Same Employer in the Past Five Years

Relocated with the same employer in the past 5 years

	Global	US	Canada	Asia	Australia /New Zealand	Middle East	Latin America	Europe
0 Times	69%	76%	69%	53%	44%	43%	53%	53%
1 Time	16%	16%	14%	16%	22%	33%	22%	19%
2+ Times	15%	8%	17%	31%	34%	24%	25%	28%

Career Path

Is there a career path for someone engaged in project/program management within your organization?

	Global	US	Canada	Asia	Australia /New Zealand	Middle East	Latin America	Europe
Yes, clearly defined and in writing	23%	22%	17%	29%	21%	32%	26%	31%
Yes, informal or unstated career path	45%	46%	55%	37%	47%	18%	40%	35%
No	32%	32%	28%	34%	32%	50%	34%	34%

Is there a career path for someone engaged in project/program management connected to roles in upper management?

	Global	US	Canada	Asia	Australia /New Zealand	Middle East	Latin America	Europe
Yes, clearly defined and in writing	24%	21%	20%	35%	22%	42%	36%	33%
Yes, informal or unstated career path	61%	64%	62%	60%	56%	50%	61%	43%
No	15%	15%	28%	5%	22%	8%	3%	25%

Does your organization have a set of performance skills (or skill sets) defined for those working in project/program management?

	Global	US	Canada	Asia	Australia /New Zealand	Middle East	Latin America	Europe
Yes, clearly defined and in writing	41%	42%	39%	35%	52%	20%	39%	50%
Yes, informal or unstated career path	31%	30%	35%	37%	27%	30%	39%	23%
No	28%	28%	27%	28%	21%	50%	22%	27%

Demographics

Location of Respondents

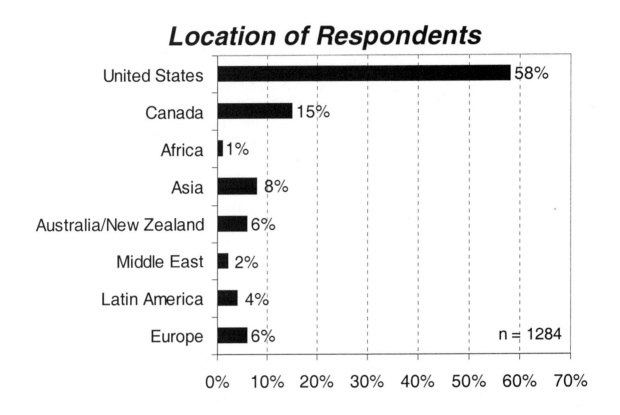

United States	58%
Canada	15%
Africa	1%
Asia	8%
Australia/New Zealand	6%
Middle East	2%
Latin America	4%
Europe	6%

n = 1284

0% 10% 20% 30% 40% 50% 60% 70%

Location of United States Respondents

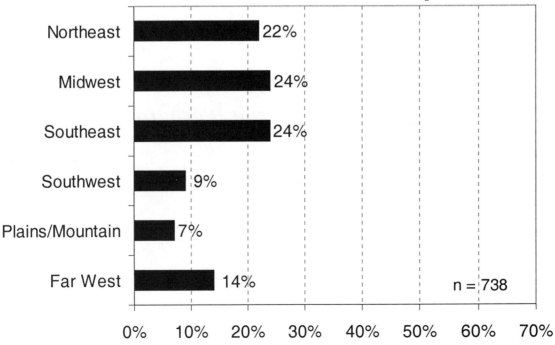

Northeast	22%
Midwest	24%
Southeast	24%
Southwest	9%
Plains/Mountain	7%
Far West	14%

n = 738

0% 10% 20% 30% 40% 50% 60% 70%

Demographics

Location of Canadian Respondents

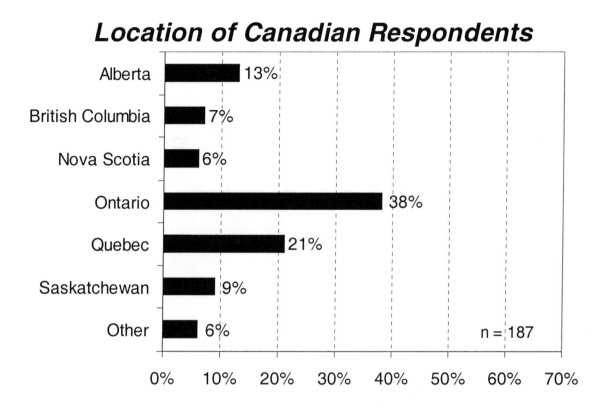

Demographics

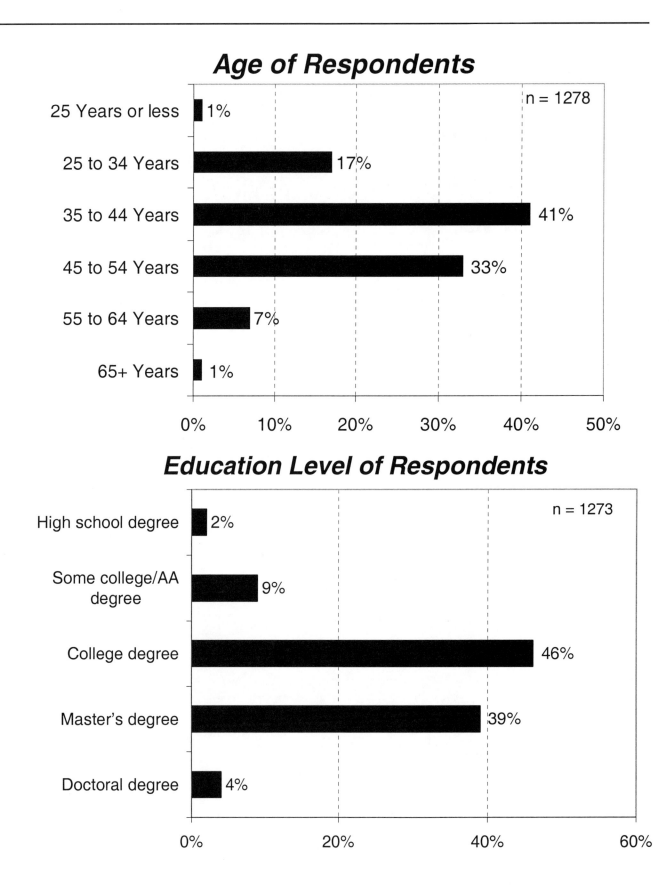

Age of Respondents

n = 1278

- 25 Years or less — 1%
- 25 to 34 Years — 17%
- 35 to 44 Years — 41%
- 45 to 54 Years — 33%
- 55 to 64 Years — 7%
- 65+ Years — 1%

0% 10% 20% 30% 40% 50%

Education Level of Respondents

n = 1273

- High school degree — 2%
- Some college/AA degree — 9%
- College degree — 46%
- Master's degree — 39%
- Doctoral degree — 4%

0% 20% 40% 60%

Demographics

Gender of Respondents

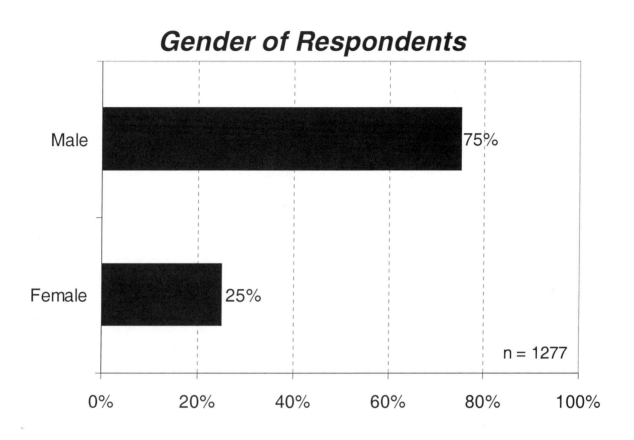

Male — 75%

Female — 25%

n = 1277

Years as a PMI Member

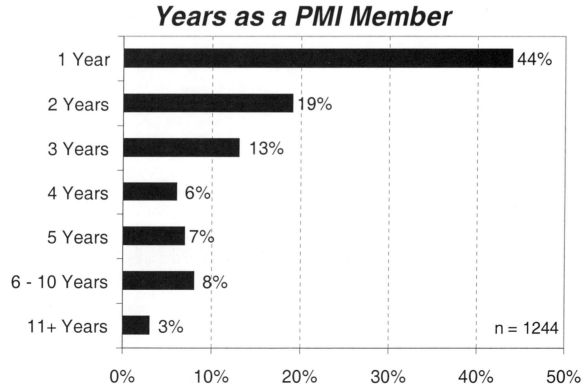

1 Year — 44%

2 Years — 19%

3 Years — 13%

4 Years — 6%

5 Years — 7%

6 - 10 Years — 8%

11+ Years — 3%

n = 1244

Survey Methods

Survey Methods

The research method involved a multi-stage, multi-sample, worldwide mail survey of PMI members. The population for the study was defined as PMI members as of March 2000. The research instrument was a collaborative effort involving PMI volunteer leaders, PMI staff, and Kerr & Downs Research. Focus groups were utilized to develop questionnaire content.

The first sample consisted of the following number of randomly selected PMI members:

> 2,500 United States members
>   500 Canada members
> <u>1,000</u> Other members
> 4,000 Total PMI members

A survey packet consisting of a questionnaire, a cover letter, and a postage-paid, return envelope was mailed to all 4,000 randomly selected PMI members on 31 March 2000. A reminder postcard was mailed to all 2,500 United States members on 11 April 2000. A second set of the complete survey packet was mailed to the following randomly selected nonrespondent PMI members on 19 April 2000.

> 1,600 United States members
>   300 Canada members
>   <u>600</u> Other members
> 2,500

Reminder telephone calls were made to 1,918 United States members between 25 April 2000 and 28 April 2000. On 28 April 2000, a broadcast fax reminder was sent to 2,500 nonresponding PMI members. On 11 May 2000 the entire questionnaire was broadcast faxed to the following number of nonresponding PMI members:

> 1,879 United States members
>   404 Canada members
>   <u>831</u> Other members
> 3,114

A separate, random sample of 3,900 PMI members was drawn in May 2000, and the questionnaire was broadcast faxed to the following on 11 May 2000:

> 1,000 United States members
>   900 Canada members
> <u>2,000</u> Other members
> 3,900

Survey Methods

A reminder fax was sent to all 3,900 individuals in the second sample on 26 May 2000. In addition to the aforementioned notifications of the survey to sample respondents, over 300 email and fax messages were sent by Kerr & Downs Research in response to sample respondents' requests.

The data collection period ended on 14 June 2000. One thousand, two hundred, and ninety (1,290) completed and usable questionnaires were returned via mail or fax. Another ninety-seven questionnaire packets were returned because of incorrect addresses. The sampling error for binomially distributed data, given a 95% confidence level, was ± 2.7%.

The 1,290 usable responses provided a survey response rate of 16%. The eight-page length of the questionnaire and the detailed nature of the information requested may have contributed to a lower than preferred response to this mail/fax survey. In order to obtain sufficient information from non-United States members, the sampling was increased in that direction. The other demographic information of the respondents was essentially consistent with the current PMI membership.

References

References

1. Project Management Insitute Educational Foundation. 1996. *Project Management Salary Survey,* 1996 Ed. Upper Darby, PA: Project Management Institute Educational Foundation.

Appendix

2000 PMI Project Management Salary Survey

> **PMI** (logo)

Instructions:
1. **Use US dollars or your country's currency when answering compensation questions.**
2. **Some questions may not apply to all PMI® members. Please answer all questions that apply to you.**

---

1. Please check (✓) the category that best reflects your employment status.

   ❏ Full-time employed   ❏ Part-time self-employed
   ❏ Full-time self-employed   ❏ Retired
   ❏ Student   ❏ Currently unemployed
   ❏ Part-time employed

2. Write in the number of hours you work in a typical week.

   _____ Hours

3. Please check the **title/position** that best fits you within your organization.

   ❏ CEO, CFO, CIO, etc.   ❏ Project Team Leader
   ❏ Senior Management   ❏ Project Coordinator
   ❏ Director of Project/Program Management   ❏ Project Planner/Scheduler
   ❏ Professor/Academic   ❏ Project Administrator
   ❏ Program Manager   ❏ Project Team Member
   ❏ Project Manager   ❏ Researcher
   ❏ Project Management Consultant/Advisor   ❏ Trainer
   ❏ Project Engineer   ❏ Other _____

4. Please describe your organization's **industry affiliation** by checking (✓) the categories that best reflect the industry focus of your organization. Please check **all** that apply.

Construction
❏ Commercial/Heavy Industrial
❏ Residential
❏ Other:
_____

Other Business Activities
❏ Academia
❏ Aerospace
❏ Architecture/Design
❏ Arts/Entertainment/Broadcasting
❏ Automation Services
❏ Business Management
   Services/Management Consulting
❏ City Management
❏ Computers/Software/DP
❏ Consulting
❏ Defense
❏ E-Business
❏ Economics/Finance
❏ Education/Training

Other Business Activities (cont.)
❏ Environmental/Waste/Sewage
❏ Engineering
❏ Financial Services
❏ Health/Human/Social Services
❏ Information Technology
❏ International Development
❏ Legal
❏ Printing/Publishing
❏ Public Administration/Government
❏ Real Estate/Insurance
❏ Recreation
❏ Supply Chain
❏ Systems Security
❏ Telecommunications
❏ Transportation
❏ Urban Development
❏ Utilities
❏ Web Technology
❏ Other:_____

Resources
❏ Agriculture
❏ Coal/Gas/Oil
❏ Ferrous Mining
❏ Forestry
❏ Non-ferrous Mining

Manufacturing
❏ Automotive
❏ Chemical
❏ Concrete/Clay/Glass/Stone
❏ Electrical/Electronic
❏ Food
❏ Machinery/Metals
❏ Paper
❏ Petroleum
❏ Pharmaceutical
❏ Plastics
❏ Textiles/Fabrics
❏ Wood
❏ Other: _____

5. Please describe your **role** within your organization.

Engineering
- ❏ Chemical
- ❏ Civil
- ❏ Electrical
- ❏ Electronics
- ❏ Environmental
- ❏ Industrial
- ❏ Mechanical
- ❏ Other:

  _____

Management
- ❏ Communications
- ❏ Configuration
- ❏ Contract/Procurement
- ❏ Corporate/Administrative

Management (cont.)
- ❏ Cost
- ❏ Critical Chain
- ❏ Earned Value
- ❏ Human Resources
- ❏ Information/Computer
- ❏ Materials
- ❏ Project/Program
- ❏ Quality
- ❏ Records
- ❏ Risk/Safety
- ❏ Scope/Technical
- ❏ Site/Facility
- ❏ Time Mgmt/Scheduling/Planning

Other
- ❏ Consulting
- ❏ Distribution
- ❏ Finance
- ❏ Financial Services
- ❏ Legal
- ❏ Marketing/Business Development/Sales
- ❏ Production
- ❏ Project Accounting/Audit
- ❏ Public Relations
- ❏ Research/Product Development
- ❏ Service & Outsourcing
- ❏ Teaching/Training
- ❏ Web Strategist/Technologist
- ❏ Other: _____

6. Please identify the scope of your responsibilities. While there is some overlap across the descriptions below, please check (✓) the description that best fits your **responsibilities** within your organization. (**Please read all descriptions before checking only one.**)

- ❏ Accountable for the strategy and performance of the overall organization or division.

- ❏ Direct responsibility of total program execution. The program typically requires accountability for a related series of projects, executed over a broad period of time, which are designed to accomplish broad goals of the program to which these individual projects contribute.

- ❏ Responsible for directing large projects or a multitude of smaller projects. Manage all aspects of project, from beginning to end, with direct accountability for project execution while leading a team, or teams, to accomplish specific objectives in a given time frame and with limited resources.

- ❏ Work within or outside of a project or program office providing support, training, and consultation to project managers and the organization. Provide support to the project or program office and facilitate process implementation.

- ❏ Combine technical expertise essential to project execution, with management of project task(s) implementation while leading task specialists.

- ❏ Typically report to Project Manager and run certain segments or critical work packages of the project. Exceptional technical capabilities and leadership role for 3-4 person teams.

- ❏ Responsible for coordinating technical activities associated with the assigned project. Usually a technical specialist residing within the organization who is not normally held accountable for the project.

- ❏ Administer or supervise support services for project. Develop, implement, and maintain project management information system that provides adequate information with which to manage the project.

- ❏ Track, coordinate and publish detailed planning and scheduling for the project.

- ❏ Team member from a functional department or project office with recognized specialty or "expert" status within the respective organization. Function as an individual contributor or serve as an interface with other specialists in respective departments.

- ❏ None of the above applies to me.

7. Check (✓) the geographic scope of the projects in which you are currently engaged or managing. (**Check All That Apply**)

- ❏ Local
- ❏ State/province
- ❏ Multi-state/province
- ❏ Within **one** country
- ❏ Multiple countries
- ❏ Multiple continents

8. Thinking of the projects in which you are now engaged or managing, please check (✓) the category that best reflects the average budget size (in US $) of the **typical** project in which you are now engaged or managing. **(See below if you wish to answer using your country's currency.)**

❑ < $100,000	❑ $3.0 million–3.99 million	❑ $100.0 million–499.99 million
❑ $100,000–249,999	❑ $4.0 million–4.99 million	❑ $500.0 million–999.99 million
❑ $250,000–499,999	❑ $5.0 million–9.99 million	❑ $1.0 billion–9.9 billion
❑ $500,000–999,999	❑ $10.0 million–24.99 million	❑ ≥ $10.0 billion
❑ $1.0 million–1.99 million	❑ $25.0 million–49.99 million	
❑ $2.0 million–2.99 million	❑ $50.0 million–99.99 million	

If you wish to answer this question using your country's currency, please write in the average budget size and write in the name of your currency:

_____ Average budget size _____ Currency (e.g., lira, pound, yen, etc.)

9. Please write in the current number of projects you are personally engaged in or managing.

a._____

10. Thinking of all the projects you are now managing, please write in the approximate number of people you presently supervise. **(This question may not apply to all PMI members.)**

a._____ Total number of people you supervise

11. Please write in the total number of employees engaged in project/program management at your office/site and in the entire organization.

_____ # of employees engaged in project/program management at your office or location or division

_____ # of employees engaged in project/program management in the entire organization

12. Please write in the total number of employees within your organization at your office/site and in the entire organization.

_____ # of employees at your office or location or division

_____ # of employees in the entire organization

13. How many years have you worked in project management?

_____ Years

14. How many years have you worked for your current employer?

_____ Years

15. Have you earned the PMP® certification?

❑ Yes
❑ No

16. Please write in the number of individuals who have earned the PMP certification at your office/site.

_____

17. Check (✓) all types of support your organization provides for those striving for PMP certification at your office/site. **(CHECK ALL THAT APPLY)**

❑ Paid leave	❑ Requires PMP certification
❑ Pay for meetings/training	❑ Rewards PMP certification
❑ Pay for examination application fee	❑ Other_____
❑ Recommends striving for PMP certification	

18. Check (✓) all types of support your organization provides to PMPs for maintaining certification at your office/site. **(CHECK ALL THAT APPLY)**

❑ Paid leave   ❑ Requires maintaining PMP certification

❑ Pay for meetings/training   ❑ Rewards maintaining PMP certification

❑ Recommends maintaining PMP® certification   ❑ Other_____

Compensation

Please note:

1. **This and all other data will be kept strictly confidential, and**
2. **If you prefer to answer in your country's currency rather than in US dollars, please write in your country and your currency below (e.g., lira, pound, yen – be specific please):**

_____ Country   _____ Currency used in Questions 19 & 20

19. For this question, please write in your:

_____ 1999 Annual salary/earnings   →   _____ % Increase/decrease since 1998

_____ 1999 Annual bonus/overtime   →   _____ % Increase/decrease since 1998

_____ 1999 Annual deferred compensation   →   _____ % Increase/decrease since 1998

20. Please indicate whether or not you receive the following benefits, and, if known, please write in the US dollar **(or country currency used in #19)** equivalent that you received in 1999.

Yes	No	Financial Value	
❑	❑	_____	All insurance (from employer and/or government)
❑	❑	_____	Retirement contributions by employer
❑	❑	_____	Performance incentive
❑	❑	_____	Retention incentive
❑	❑	_____	Signing bonus
❑	❑	_____	Stock options
❑	❑	_____	Relocation/travel bonus
❑	❑	_____	Holiday bonus
❑	❑	_____	Housing allowance/free housing
❑	❑	_____	Free participation in stock purchases
❑	❑	_____	Vehicle
❑	❑	_____	Entertainment allowance
❑	❑	_____	Club memberships
❑	❑	_____	Tickets to cultural events, sporting events, etc.
❑	❑	_____	At-risk bonus pay
❑	❑	_____	Mortgage paid by employer until current house sold
❑	❑	_____	Other benefits that have a financial value Please list: _____ _____

Retirement

21. If you or your employer have a retirement plan, what is it?

   - ❏ No retirement plan **(Skip to 23)**
   - ❏ Defined benefit
   - ❏ Defined contribution
   - ❏ IRA
   - ❏ Money purchase plan
   - ❏ 401 (k)-type plan – employee only
   - ❏ 401 (k)-type plan – employer match

   - ❏ Profit sharing
   - ❏ Simplified employee plan (SEP)
   - ❏ Supplementary executive plan
   - ❏ Tax sheltered annuity
   - ❏ Employee stock options
   - ❏ Flexible benefit plan
   - ❏ Other, please list

22. How long is the vesting period before you become eligible for retirement benefits?

   - ❏ No vesting period
   - ❏ 6 months
   - ❏ 1 year
   - ❏ 2 years

   - ❏ 3–5 years
   - ❏ > 5 years
   - ❏ Other, please list

   _____

Insurance

23. For each type of insurance listed below, please:

   a. Check (✓) if you receive it from your employer (or from your government).
   b. Write in percent of premium paid by your employer (or government).
   c. Answer related questions where appropriate.

Offered by Your Employer or Government			Percent of Premium Paid by Employer or Government	Related Questions
Yes	No			
❏	❏	Healthcare insurance	_____ %	Effective after _____ days Amount of deductible $_____
❏	❏	Long-term disability	_____ %	Effective after _____ days
❏	❏	Short-term disability	_____ %	Effective after _____ days
❏	❏	Accidental death	_____ %	
❏	❏	Vision insurance	_____ %	
❏	❏	Prescription drugs	_____ %	
❏	❏	Dental insurance	_____ %	
❏	❏	Life insurance	_____ %	Amount of coverage $_____
❏	❏	Professional liability	_____ %	
❏	❏	Other: _____ _____	_____ % _____ %	

Paid Leave

24. Please write in the number of days of paid leave to which you were entitled in 1999.

Paid Days

_____ Vacation (holiday)

_____ Sick days

_____ Holidays (Malvinas Day, Bastille Day, Boxing Day, Memorial Day,
                National Day, Constitution Memorial Day, etc.)

_____ Personal days

_____ Other days, please describe _____

Benefits

25. Please check (✓) each of the benefits you receive from your employer (or from your government).

❏ Paid child care   ❏ Free parking

❏ Maternity (paternity) leave   ❏ Adult dependent care

❏ Matched savings   ❏ Cellular telephone

❏ Sabbatical with pay   ❏ Laptop/home computer

❏ Wellness program   ❏ Other, please specify: _____

26. Concerning insurance and other types of benefits covered in questions 20 through 25, does your employer offer you a standard plan (a fixed set of benefits) or a cafeteria plan (you are allowed to choose a certain number of benefits up to a given monetary value)?

❏ Standard plan

❏ Cafeteria plan

❏ Other, please specify _____

27. Please write in the percentage of the expenses/fees that your organization reimburses for each of the following. **(Write "0" if there is no reimbursement.)**

*Percent Reimbursed
by Your Employer*

Academic tuition   _____ %

Professional seminars/workshops   _____ %

Professional association dues   _____ %

Work Environment

28. Is your **primary** work environment a traditional office, a virtual office (on the road), or an office in your home or residence?

❏ Traditional office   ❏ Office in home or residence

❏ Virtual office   ❏ Other, please specify _____

29. In a typical month, how many days are you away from your primary work location?

_____ Days

30. If you work primarily in a virtual office, how satisfied are you with this arrangement?

- ❏ Very satisfied
- ❏ Satisfied
- ❏ Somewhat satisfied
- ❏ Somewhat dissatisfied
- ❏ Dissatisfied
- ❏ Very dissatisfied

31. If you work primarily from an office in your home, for which of the following expenses do you receive financial support? **(Check all that apply.)**

- ❏ Home/laptop computer
- ❏ Cell phone
- ❏ Extra telephone line
- ❏ Other, please specify _____

32. In the past 5 years, how many times have you:

_____ Changed employers

_____ Relocated with the same employer

Career Path

33. Is there a career path for someone engaged in project or program management within your organization?

- ❏ Yes ⟶ Clearly defined and in writing
- ❏ Yes ⟶ Informal or unstated career path
- ❏ No **(Skip to 35)**

34. Is the career path for someone engaged in project or program management connected to roles in upper management?

- ❏ Yes ⟶ Clearly defined and in writing
- ❏ Yes ⟶ Informal or unstated
- ❏ No

35. Please write in the title of your immediate supervisor.

_____

36. Does your organization have a set of performance skills (or skill sets) defined for those working in project or program management?

- ❏ Yes ⟶ Clearly defined and in writing
- ❏ Yes ⟶ Informal or unstated
- ❏ No

Profile

37. Check (✓) the category that reflects your age.

- ❏ < 25
- ❏ 25 to 34
- ❏ 35 to 44
- ❏ 45 to 54
- ❏ 55 to 64
- ❏ 65 or older

38. Please check (✓) the highest formal education level you have obtained.

    ❏ High school degree or equivalent   ❏ Master's degree or equivalent

    ❏ Some college/AA degree or equivalent   ❏ Doctoral degree or equivalent

    ❏ College degree or equivalent

39. Please write in your major field of study for your degree.

    _____

40. How many years have you been a PMI member?

    _____ Years

41. Are you male or female?

    ❏ Male
    ❏ Female

42. Please write in the state/province and country in which your office is located.

    _____   _____

Thank you for completing this questionnaire. If you have any questions, please contact Phillip E. Downs, Ph.D. (pd@kerr-downs.com or +850-906-3111).

Instructions for Returning Survey

1. After completing this survey, complete "The 2000 PMI Project Management Salary Survey" form enclosed with the survey.
2. Please fax your survey and form back to Kerr & Downs Research at the fax number indicated on your cover letter.

5566 ↑